Key Trial CONTROL TACTICS: A Guide to Winning the ULTIMATE VERDICT

Volume I

Mark A. Dombroff, Esq.

EXECUTIVE REPORTS CORPORATION
Englewood Cliffs, NJ

Library of Congress Cataloging in Publication Data

Dombroff, Mark A.
Key trial control tactics.

Includes index.
1. Trial practice—United States. I. Title.
KF8915.D56 1982 347.73'7 82-15510
ISBN 0-13-514851-0 347.3077

What This Guide Will Do For You

The key to winning a case is *controlling* its progress. But where does an attorney find the techniques, strategies and tactics needed to do this?

That is why I have written this Guide. It is a practical manual aimed at the experienced lawyer who wants immediate access to the newest, best and most effective methods of trial control known today. The procedures, techniques and tactics it contains have just one goal—to help you seize control of each case right from the beginning—and keep control right through to the *ultimate* verdict.

All of the methods in this Guide have had their worth proven time and time again in the courtroom, and have been refined by repeated use.

Here, in short, are the key trial control tactics especially developed for civil litigation, but which are crucial to the effective and successful handling of *any* type of case.

In this Guide, you'll discover:

- How to prepare and conduct direct examination to produce the results you want, in a way that minimizes risks on cross-examination.
- How to use powerful cross-examination tactics and techniques that will neatly take control of your opponent's witnesses and quickly discredit them.
- How to select expert witnesses, qualify them, and add the maximum amount of credibility to their testimony.
- How to make an opening statement that puts you in immediate command of the case and quickly gains the confidence and sympathy of the jury and judge.
- How to make the most productive use of demonstrative evidence during a trial, including models, videotape, charts, graphs and even computer-generated evidence.
- How to organize and prepare for trial in a way that lets you and not your opponent set the rules.

- How to develop and present psychologically "right" closing arguments that make all the pieces fit together—and lead to the one inevitable conclusion you want.
- How to use special techniques for proving and winning the damages portion of a tort case, and setting the highest possible dollar value on them.
- How to seize control at deposition hearings—and start demolishing your opponent's case right then and there.
- How to develop an arsenal of powerful post-trial tactics, strategies, plans and techniques to keep control—and guarantee that the ultimate verdict will continue to be in your favor.

. . . plus many other trial control techniques and tactics presented in a logical, useful and easy-to-find format, all keyed to the litigative process.

They all have one thing in common—each and every one is geared to make *you* the lawyer who writes the ground rules upon which the case is prepared and tried—and to give you a decided advantage over your opponent.

In trial practice, as in many other fields of endeavor, experience is the best teacher. In my own development as a trial lawyer, I have found that the best trial advice comes from the experience of others.

What is set forth in this Guide is representative not only of my own years as a civil litigator, but also of the collective experiences of those dozens of trial lawyers with whom I have been fortunate enough to collaborate and, in some cases, oppose.

To this material, I have added a host of checklists and model forms that I have developed and used for many years. Their value has been proven many times over, and they greatly amplify the effectiveness of the techniques and procedures you will find in these pages.

Also included are excerpts and examples from actual trials, so that you can see how well these trial control methods work in action.

Keeping in mind that no two lawsuits are the same, the tactics and techniques within this Guide comprise a framework upon which you may effectively master, prepare and present your case in court, seize and keep *control* of the case's progress, and win the *ultimate* verdict each time. Use the Guide wisely, and it will serve you well.

Mark A. Dombroff, Esq.

Summary Table of Contents—Volume I

[Detailed tables of contents appear on the first page of each chapter.]

Summary Table of Contents—Volume II

[Detailed tables of contents appear on the first page of each chapter.]

About the Author

Mark A. Dombroff is Director of the Torts Branch, Civil Division, United States Department of Justice, and is responsible for managing offices in San Francisco, New York, and Washington. His varied experience includes the trial, to a successful conclusion, of a landmark aircrash case, resulting in the complete exoneration of the United States and a finding of willful misconduct against the air carrier.

Mr. Dombroff is a prolific author, who writes a regular column on government litigation for *The National Law Journal,* and has published numerous articles in *Trial Lawyer's Guide, Flying* magazine, and the *Legal Times of Washington.* He is also the author of a forthcoming book on demonstrative evidence. He lectures throughout the country for ATLA and for the Practising Law Institute, and teaches at Antioch University.

1

How To Increase the Prospects for Controlling Your Case and Winning the Ultimate Verdict

Table of Contents

1

How To Increase the Prospects for Controlling Your Case and Winning the Ultimate Verdict

LAYING THE GROUND WORK FOR TRIAL VICTORY

A trial, with the preparation which goes into it, bears a striking similarity to a theatrical production. Just as a good script, good actors and many rehearsals make a good play, pretrial discovery, preparation and organization are keys to a successful trial.

Unlike a play, a trial has only one "opening night" and only one chance to get "favorable reviews," be they from a judge or a jury. It is your responsibility as a trial lawyer—writer, producer and director—to ensure that your play—the trial—is prepared and organized to ensure the most effective presentation.

As a frequent lecturer on trial practice subjects, I stress the importance of proper preparation out of court and frequently comment that a case is either won or lost before a lawyer ever sets foot in the courtroom. While this is not a scientific statement, it is based upon experience. Unless you fully and properly prepare yourself for trial, you will do yourself, your case and, most importantly, your client a disservice.

A TRIAL PREPARATION CHECKLIST

A trial preparation checklist is an invaluable aid that can guide you through all aspects of trial preparation. There is nothing worse than realizing, on the eve of trial, that you forgot to accomplish something. The use of the following checklist serves as a case management tool. While not all of the tasks need be accomplished for each case, the categories covered are comprehensive.

TRIAL PREPARATION CHECKLIST

Case: ______________________________

	In Progress	Completed	Filed
1. Preparation of required or necessary pleadings:			
A. Witness list			
B. Exhibit list			
C. Proposed voir dire questions			
D. Trial brief			
E. Evidentiary memorandum			
F. Motions in limine			
G. Proposed jury instructions			
H. Findings of fact			
I. Conclusions of law			

	In Progress	Completed	Filed
J. Expert witness qualifications			
2. Preparation of trial materials:			
A. Development of evidence			
1. Client/witness interviews			
2. Investigations			
3. Consultations			
4. Scientific testing and aids			
5. Expert appraisals and analysis			
6. Witness selection and information			
7. View of the scene			
8. Theory of the case			
a. Trial strategy			
b. Trial techniques			
c. Alternate theories			
d. Evidentiary theories			
B. Exhibits			
1. Direct evidence			
2. Demonstrative evidence			
C. Trial notebook			
D. Opening statements			
E. Closing statements			
F. Direct exam and cross-exam questions			
1. Interviews			
a. Lay witnesses			
1. Direct-exam			
2. Cross-exam			

	In Progress	Completed	Filed
b. Expert witnesses			
1. Direct and cross-exam			
2. Consultation			
2. Review of discovery materials			
3. Review of source materials			
G. Familiarity with judge			
3. Organization for trial:			
A. Exhibits			
1. Marking			
2. Copies			
3. Familiarity			
4. Witness-exhibit sequence			
B. Discovery materials			
1. Summaries			
2. Indexing			
3. Pretrial determinations and rulings for trial use			
C. Witness and exhibit logistics			
D. Documents			
1. Indexing and cross-indexing			
2. Summaries			
E. Witness sequence			
F. Exhibit sequence			
G. Trial use of discovery materials			

THE DISCOVERY, PLEADING AND PRACTICE MEMORANDUM: AN EFFECTIVE DEVICE FOR CONTROLLING THE CASE

Tort litigation is an area of trial practice that produces factually complex case files. The case files are usually made up of a combination of the results of production, interrogatories, requests for admissions and deposition transcripts. The task you will have to confront is how to effectively plan for and implement the case in a manner which positions you to control the case to the maximum extent possible. The pleading and practice memorandum presents just such a vehicle.

You will do your client and yourself a disservice if you are not being perceived by the judge as highly organized and in control. If the judge begins the trial with the preconceived notion that you are in command of the case, organized and an innovative litigator, an atmosphere will be created which is most receptive to the favorable presentation of your case.

How to Gain Control Via the Memorandum

The discovery, pleading and practice memorandum is a pleading, filed either in the form of a "Motion Seeking a Discovery, Pleading and Practice Order" or as a "Memorandum In Re: Discovery, Pleading and Practice," which have several complementary purposes, all of which are aimed at maximizing the effective preparation and presentation of your case.

1. It sets out several suggested pretrial procedures that the judge can adopt to expedite the pretrial and trial proceedings in your case.
2. It distinguishes you as the party seeking to move the case along using a series of innovative procedures.

3. It provides a vehicle for your pretrial and trial procedures to be adopted over those proposed by your opponent.
4. It places a burden on your opponent to accept, reject or come up with alternative procedures.

Too often inexperienced trial lawyers tend to litigate on an ad hoc basis without giving enough long-term thought to future phases of the litigation until it is too late to do anything but react. If you use long-term planning in making judgments as to the course of action which the case should take, you are in a decidedly better position to control what happens. The pleading and practice memorandum can be utilized towards better achieving that end.

What to Include for Greater Control: The memorandum should be filed as a memorandum or as a motion. Some or all of the following provisions may be included as desirable in the context of your specific case.

IN THE * * * COURT
FOR THE (DISTRICT)(STATE) OF * * *

	)	
	)	
Caption	)	Memorandum of the [Plaintiff or
	)	Defendant, as appropriate] In Re:
	)	Discovery, Pleading And Practice
	)	
	)	

Introduction

The [plaintiff or defendant, as appropriate] for the purpose of expediting the pretrial preparation and trial of this action, suggests the adoption of the following procedures for the discovery, pretrial and trial aspects of this litigation.

The introductory language is purely a matter of style. One of the advantages of making a motion seeking a discovery, pleading and practice order is that your opponent and the judge are required to act. If a motion is filed, the introductory language would obviously be different. One form it might take is as follows:

> Please take notice that the [plaintiff, defendant] moves this Honorable Court to enter an order on discovery, pleading and practice in this matter.
>
> Attached hereto and filed in support hereof is a memorandum and a proposed order.
>
> 1. Discovery in the liability and damages aspects of the case should be bifurcated with separate discovery being permitted, pursuant to local rules, for each aspect of the case.

Control Tactic: You should also consider other types of bifurcations or severances, e.g., parties, issues. Obviously if such are suggested, you should include requests for separate discovery with respect to each party or issue.

Most rules of procedure, both state and federal, provide the court with a broad range of discretion in allowing separate trials of any claim, cross-claim, counterclaim, or third-party claim, or of any separate issue or any number of claims, cross-claims, counterclaims, third-party claims or issues. Furthermore, if a local rule exists which limits the number of depositions, interrogatories or admissions, severance or bifurcation may also allow for expanded discovery if separate discovery is provided for in each separate part of the case.

> 2. Whenever a party has an objection to responding to either an interrogatory, a request for production or a request for admission, all answers or documents that are not objec-

tionable will be filed and/or served as appropriate. Simultaneously, the objection(s) will be filed and served with all legal and factual arguments in support of the objection. Also filed at this time, but *in camera* only, will be the objectionable response or document.

If the objection goes to the voluminous nature of the information sought, no *in camera* submission need be made initially. However, counsel should submit affidavits attesting to the voluminous nature of material being sought.

Within five days of receipt of the objection and supporting authorities, opposing counsel will file a response. The court, with or without argument or further briefing as it may deem appropriate, may then rule upon the objections without further delay and if it overrules them, make the responsive information immediately available to counsel. Following this procedure should substantially expedite the discovery process and aid in making counsel more responsive to discovery requests.

This procedure is one which was developed for complex tort litigation. While imposing a burden on you as well as your opponent, it does have the effect of substantially expediting that phase of discovery surrounding objections.

Obviously, where an objection is based on the voluminous nature of the information sought, the very act of providing it to the court *in camera* defeats the objection. Under such circumstances, an *in camera* inspection would not be accomplished.

3. Pursuant to an order of this court, a Special Master should be appointed to preside over all discovery with full power to exercise all powers granted by the rules of procedure, and such additional powers as are usually exercised by Special Masters. The expenses of the Master should be borne equally by the parties with the accumulated costs to be assessed against the losing party at the conclusion of the proceedings.

Obviously, you should reserve the use of a master for those unusual cases where the discovery process will be either so broad or, due to personalities of counsel, so difficult as to require some continued judicial presence and control. Such cases are usually, and thankfully, the exception.

> 4. In order to minimize the repetitive use of damage interrogatories, plaintiff(s) should be required to provide damage information within 10 days of the filing of their complaint.

This procedure is most effectively utilized in the multi-party case.

> 5. For the purpose of expediting discovery and minimizing cost—unless the court manifests a contrary desire—all status conferences, motion hearings, and preliminary pretrials should be handled via telephone.

This procedure does nothing other than track a trend that is becoming more and more predominant.

> 6. In order to simplify the handling of documents and exhibits both during discovery and trial, the use of a consecutive numbering system, without regard to which party produces or offers a document, should be observed. By doing so, reference to documents will be simplified inasmuch as that document marked, for example, as exhibit 3 in the Jones deposition will always be exhibit 3, be it in subsequent depositions or at trial.

The benefit of this procedure is self-evident. If adopted, no longer are there multiple exhibits bearing the same number which, assuming re-numbering is required by local rule for trial, is inconsistent with the references to the exhibit in the deposition. Obviously, such a procedure, in order to be maximally effective, should be followed from the outset of the litigation and, for that reason, should be suggested early.

In order to accommodate exhibits marked at trial (e.g., exhibits used on cross-examination and not pre-marked, demonstrative exhibits, court-marked exhibits, etc.), blocks of numbers can be reserved for each party (e.g., 1–1000 would be for pre-marked exhibits, 1001–2000 for plaintiff's trial exhibits, 2001–3000 for defendant's trial exhibits, etc.).

If your local rules require re-numbering for trial (e.g., numbers for plaintiff, letters for defendant), you may require leave of court to utilize a single sequential numbering system.

> 7. To the maximum extent practicable and in lieu of the verbatim reading of depositions at trial, either straight narratives of proffered deposition testimony, or a combination of narrative and verbatim extracts, should be utilized. The party intending to offer deposition testimony will have the obligation of preparing the narrative which will then be submitted to opposing counsel for additions and/or objections. Those objections, to either form or substance, which cannot be resolved by counsel will be referred to the court for resolution.
>
> A similar procedure will be utilized in the event either party intends to rely upon voluminous documentary evidence for the preparation of summaries.

How to Make Effective Use of Summaries: This procedure is especially effective if you expect to have to rely upon a large amount of deposition testimony or documentary evidence. The basic requirements for using summaries in litigation are:

1. The proof(s) involve the contents of voluminous writings, recordings or photographs;

2. The documents involved cannot conveniently be examined in court; and
3. The originals, or duplicates, are made available to opposing counsel for examination at a reasonable time and place.

In order to maximize the effective use of summaries, you should keep in mind several practical guidelines:

1. Summaries must be accurate.
2. Summaries should be prepared as far in advance of trial as possible. If possible, you should use them at depositions and have them authenticated.
3. If not utilized prior to the start of trial, your opponent should be given ample opportunity to review the summaries and underlying documents.
4. Pretrial stipulations on accuracy and admissibility should be sought. One effective means of doing this is through requests for admission directed at the underlying documents as well as the summaries themselves.
5. In the absence of an overwhelming volume of underlying material, the underlying documents or depositions should be offered into evidence.
6. Have both large (if possible, 4′ by 6′) and small (8½″ by 11″) versions prepared. By having both sizes, the judge and jury can follow along with either you or the witness when the summary is used.
7. Summaries should be simple and straightforward, requiring as little interpretation by the judge and jury as possible.

A Special Point About Deposition Summaries: With respect to deposition summaries, prior to trial you should prepare a narrative summary of desired deposition testimony including, where appropriate, verbatim excerpts. In many ways such a narrative reads like an offer of proof without qualifying language. Thus, a narrative summary of an eyewitness to an auto accident might read:

> On Jan. 13, 1980, at 8 P.M., Michael Parks was walking across Elm Avenue. On that date, Mr. Parks was 32 years old and in good health with 20/20 vision. . . .

The proposed narrative is given to opposing counsel who supplements it with additions and/or notes corrections or objections. You then note your objections to the additions or changes. Whatever you cannot resolve with your opponent is brought to the court for final resolution and ruling.

These suggested procedures for inclusion in the memorandum really only scratch the surface of devices that may be used to expedite and more effectively organize a tort case. Your own experience and practice will undoubtedly provide additional devices which are suitable for inclusion. Remember, the central purpose of this memorandum is, in addition to suggesting proven procedures for more effectively and efficiently preparing and presenting a case, to cast you in the role of innovator and attorney in control of the litigation.

TRIAL BRIEFS

You should always file a trial brief. As an adversary, you must do everything and anything you can to put your case in front of the judge in a persuasive fashion. Even in a jury trial, the attitude of the judge manifests itself in rulings both before and during trial. The more you can do to educate the judge prior to trial regarding you, your case and your version of the facts, the better the chances of having your positions adapted.

When Should You File Your Trial Brief?

A trial brief should be filed in sufficient time to permit the judge to read and consider it, but not so far in advance of trial that you permit opposing counsel to either respond to it or file one he had not otherwise intended to. For example, if a trial begins on a Monday, the filing of your trial brief on the preceding Wednesday or Thursday with, in addition to normal service copies, a copy delivered directly to the judge's chambers is not an unrealistic timetable—it gives the judge sufficient time to read the brief, but it minimizes the time available to your opponent to respond.

What Should Your Trial Brief Contain?

A trial brief, remembering that its purpose is to educate the judge, is not unlike a road map or the program to a play. Just as the map or program are essentially previews of what is to come, a trial brief serves a similar purpose. However, a trial brief must persuade the reader of the correctness of your position. As a result, it should be carefully drafted so that the judge relies upon it as he would a map or a program, to get his bearings at any given time and aid him in getting where he is going.

Keeping this purpose in mind, an effective trial brief should be structured along the following lines.

IN THE * * * COURT
FOR THE (DISTRICT)(STATE) OF * * *

	)	
	)	
CAPTION	)	Plaintiff's or Defendant's
	)	[as appropriate] Trial Brief
	)	

I. *FACTS*
The factual discussion should be as complete as possible with citations to the source of the facts (e.g., depositions, admissions, documents, etc.). The slant of the factual statement should be adversarial and put as favorable an interpretation

on them as fairness permits. Remember, you want the judge to utilize your brief as a yardstick against which he measures what is unfolding in the courtroom.

Too many lawyers do not recognize the persuasive potential of a clearly written factual statement. Do not fall into the trap of giving short shrift to the facts in favor of the law. By far, most tort actions are factual disputes whose successful resolution depend on an interpretation of the facts that are favorable to your client.

II. *APPLICABLE LAW*

In this section you should attempt to parallel, relative to the law, what you have done in section I relative to the facts. The court should have presented to it, in a persuasive format, the law as you would have it applied to your case. Included within this section should be citations and, where appropriate, excerpts from cases. If there is a case, or a number of cases, which are especially favorable to your position, they should be appended to the trial brief for easy reference by the court.

III. *FACTUAL ISSUES*

Careful attention should be given to framing the factual issues in a manner which gives your position the best chance of prevailing.

For example, assume you represent a merchant in a slip-and-fall action which has, as a central issue, the existence or non-existence of a pool of water in the vicinity of the fall. Representing the plaintiff in this action, an effective framing of this issue might be, "Was the defendant negligent in permitting a pool of water to accumulate on the floor in the area where the plaintiff slipped and fell?"

If the issue is framed in this fashion and accepted by the court, the defendant is effectively faced with overcoming the presumption that water was on the floor and that the only remaining issue is one of negligence.

Your task in framing the factual issues is to cause the judge to accept your version of what occurred. By doing so, you are in a position to be able to subtly influence evidentiary rulings, instructions to the jury and, hopefully, the outcome of the case.

IV. *LEGAL ISSUES*

In much the same way as you present the factual issues in the preceding section in a fashion calculated to maximize their likely resolution in your favor, a similar approach is taken in this section relative to the legal issues.

V. *WITNESSES*

Accompanying each witness's name and identity should be a brief summary of the element(s) of the case to which that witness will testify.

VI. *EXHIBITS*

Exhibits are frequently the central evidence in any case. Since the philosophy of civil litigation has done away with the concept of "trial by ambush," all exhibits must usually be made available to opposing counsel prior to trial. The only exception which you will typically find to this broad rule relates to exhibits used for cross-examination, including impeachment, or rebuttal. Similarly, many rules require the completion and submission to the court of exhibit lists prior to trial. This section of the trial brief should contain a listing of all exhibits required to be disclosed. It would also be a good idea, notwithstanding local rules, to include as an attachment to the trial brief an exhibit list for the use of the court during trial. Sufficient copies should also be available for the court reporter, court clerk, law clerk and opposing counsel.

The format you should utilize in an exhibit list for the judge is as follows:

COURT NAME
(e.g., In the _____ Court for the
(State)(District) of _______)

	)	
	)	
Caption	)	Civil Number
	)	
	)	

(PLAINTIFF'S)(DEFENDANT'S) EXHIBIT LIST

Exhibit Number	Description	Date Marked For Identification	Date Received Evidence
________	________	________	________
________	________	________	________
________	________	________	________
________	________	________	________

Practice Tip: Blank exhibit lists can be prepared and simply filled in with the information appropriate to your case.

Gain Greater Control with an Appendix: In addition to the foregoing, there are frequently cases, both published and unpublished, which you want the judge to read. Citing them in your brief makes the judge aware of their existence, however the inclusion of an appendix of legal materials to your brief which includes important cases is frequently one way of ensuring that the judge will read the case. This is especially true if you are arguing a legal point prior to or during trial. The ability to point out to the judge that the appendix to your trial brief contains the case you are then discussing will frequently result in the judge relying on your trial brief to a much greater extent.

Remember, just as you use a map on a trip when you are unfamiliar with the route, a trial brief serves the same function. It permits the judge to preview the trip upon which you are about to embark and gives him a frame of reference to which to relate your position and against which to measure your opponent.

HOW A TRIAL BOOK CAN HELP PROVE YOUR CASE

Even the simplest automobile accident case frequently involves a number of witnesses, technical terms, chronology of events and maps. The simplicity of a case of this type may be obscured by what seems to be a high degree of confusion in or the volume of the factual evidence.

Your task in such circumstances is to be able to assist both the judge and jury in understanding the facts and in identifying and organizing the evidence in a fashion which makes it most likely that you will win. Both a pleading and practice memorandum as well as a trial brief assist in these goals. A trial book can be of further assistance.

In its simplest form, a trial book may consist of a glossary of technical terms including definitions, a listing of individuals and witnesses with a sentence or two explaining their role in the case and copies of any agreed upon key exhibits.

An excerpt from the trial book in an aviation tort case follows.

NAMES OF INDIVIDUALS AND WITNESSES WHO WILL BE MENTIONED IN THE TRIAL

Harold Anderson: Mr. Anderson is a Flight Standards specialist employed by the FAA and participated in the design of the ILS/DME approach at the Pago Pago Airport.

William A. Arnett: Mr. Arnett was a technician employed by the FAA at Pago Pago.

Captain Howard W. Ashcraft: Captain Ashcraft was the senior Pan American captain assigned to the Pan American group assisting the National Transportation Safety Board in its investigation of the crash of Flight 806.

Frank D. Bateman, Jr.: Mr. Bateman was the controller on duty in the CAPIS during the time that Flight 806 was on the approach.

James A. Boetcher: Mr. Boetcher was an FAA electronics technician assigned to Pago Pago who performed maintenance on the instrument landing system there.

☆ ☆ ☆ ☆

GLOSSARY OF TERMS WHICH WILL BE MENTIONED IN THE TRIAL

Absolute Altitude: True altitude above the actual surface of the earth, either land or water.

Advisory Circular (AC): A series of external FAA publications consisting of all non-regulatory material of a policy, guidance and informational nature.

Air Carrier: A person who undertakes directly by lease, or other arrangement, to engage in air transportation. (FAR Part 1.)

Air Carrier Airport: An airport (or runway) designated by design and/or use for air carrier operation.

Air Carrier—Certified Route: An air carrier holding a Certificate of Public Convenience and Necessity issued by the Civil Aeronautics Board to conduct scheduled services over specified routes and a limited amount of non-scheduled operations.

Aircraft Configuration: A term referring to the relative position of the various elements affecting the aerodynamic characteristics of an aircraft.

Airframe: The fuselage, booms, nacelles, cowlings, fairings, airfoil surfaces (including rotors, but excluding propellers and rotating airfoils of engines), and landing gear of an aircraft and their accessories and controls.

☆ ☆ ☆ ☆

How to Present the Trial Book to the Jury: The trial book is especially valuable in a jury case. Where you and your opponent have agreed and stipulated to its contents, a copy should be given to each juror immediately after opening statements along with an explanatory statement by the judge. In effect, the contents of the jury book becomes stipulated facts in the case which are readily accessible to the jurors as needed throughout the trial.

Below is an example of the instructions that might be given to the jury regarding the trial book:

> Ladies and gentlemen of the jury, in order to assist you in understanding the evidence, counsel have prepared what we call a jury book. Contained within it, and we have a copy for each of you, are exhibits which all counsel agree are important to the case as well as a glossary of certain terms which you will hear repeatedly throughout the trial. Also in the book is a list of names of witnesses who will testify at trial along with a brief explanation of who they are. This is included to help you keep the cast of characters straight.

Each morning this book will be given to you and each evening the clerk will collect them.

In a non-jury case, a trial book can be of equal value although the contents can be easily incorporated or added to your trial brief. In the event you are not able to obtain the agreement of your opponent to the contents of a joint trial book, you always have the option of including as appendices within your trial brief a glossary of terms, your "who's who" in the case and copies of pertinent exhibits.

2

Making an Opening Statement That Puts You in Fast Command of the Case

Table of Contents

2

Making an Opening Statement That Puts You in Fast Command of the Case

WHAT SHOULD AN OPENING STATEMENT ACHIEVE?

I have frequently heard it said that lawyers are on trial just as much as their clients. Just as frequently, I have heard that juries make up their minds during opening statements and that very few individual jurors change their minds during the course of a trial. Regardless of how much truth you attribute to these statements, an opening statement must get and keep the confidence of the jury. This confidence must be placed not only in the case, but also in you as the attorney presenting that case.

An opening statement is the first time during the trial of a case that you are able to address the jury and the judge. While you may have had other opportunities to come before the judge on discovery matters or motions, all of the issues presented to the judge in those situations were typically limited to the narrow issues you were then discussing.

The trial presents the culmination of all prior decisions in the context of the facts of the case. The opening statement is the first opportunity which you have to set the stage for what is to follow.

In order to be successful, an opening statement must achieve several things:

1. Obtain the confidence of the jury in you and your case;
2. Establish you as the lawyer in command of the case;
3. Establish you as the lawyer who can be turned to for the definitive version of what occurred;
4. Convince the jury that you are acting in good faith; and
5. Lay a foundation for the ultimate verdict.

HOW DOES AN OPENING STATEMENT ACHIEVE ITS GOALS?

To achieve its goals, an opening statement must fulfill several purposes.

Informs

An opening statement informs the judge and jury of what you will prove during the balance of your case.

- A successful opening statement should concisely narrate the facts of the case.
- You should not present facts which you know you are not going to be able to prove.
- The presentation of the facts during the opening statement should not be equivocal. You should not state "We believe the evidence will show . . ." or "We expect the evidence will show. . . ."

- It is far more effective to be definite in order to inspire confidence among the jury. Accordingly, you should indicate "The evidence will show . . ." or "We will prove. . . ."

Sets the Theme

The opening statement should set the theme for your case. By this I mean you should plant the seed of your best central idea during your opening statement. Take, for example, the theme of the "careless plaintiff."

> "Ladies and gentlemen, this case, as counsel for the plaintiff has stated is about negligence, but not the negligence of my client. Rather it is about the negligence of the plaintiff. The negligence of the plaintiff . . . the careless plaintiff. The plaintiff who didn't watch where she was walking . . . the careless plaintiff. The plaintiff who slipped because she didn't see the curb . . . the careless plaintiff. The plaintiff who now comes before you and says it's my client's fault . . . the careless plaintiff."

The unique, strong central idea of your case is the "careless plaintiff." As a result, during your opening statement, you emphasize that phrase and bring it home to the jury as the yardstick against which they should measure the allegations of the "careless plaintiff" and the conduct of your client.

Explains

The opening statement should explain the order of proof. For example, if the plaintiff has the burden and goes first, this should be explained. On the other hand, if the plaintiff's case is stipulated, the defendant may go first and this change should be explained. By the same token, with respect to assertions by the defendant of contributory negligence or counter-claims by the defendant, the shifting burden of proof and how it works should be explained.

The concept of burden of proof can be very confusing to the layperson who has been educated about the judicial process through the mass media. Only by explaining how the law shifts the burden of proof depending upon the position of the party making the allegations can the jury keep in mind why a party is attempting to do something that might otherwise seem to be inconsistent with their preconceived notions of what should be done.

Previews

The opening statement should preview what witnesses will say when they testify. In accomplishing this task during the opening statement:

- Do not detail the testimony of witnesses.
- Identify any tentative witnesses.
- Explain the use of opposing parties' testimony.
- Prepare the judge and jury for expert witnesses by explaining who they will be and what their role is in your case.
- Introduce your client and/or your key witness to the jury by pointing them out during your opening statement. With respect to your client, he or she should stand and make eye contact with the jury. With respect to witnesses who may be in the courtroom, you should simply gesture towards them and situate them in such a position so it is apparent to the judge and jury who they are.
- Explain the purpose of depositions, and how they will be used during presentation of the case.

Admits

Admit all the facts you can during your opening statement.

Admissions can oftentimes preclude the admissibility of prejudicial testimony that will have an adverse effect upon your case. In addition, admission of the facts can clear the air for the real issues to be decided in the case.

Defines

Explain technical terms that are likely to be heard by the jury. However, do not over-explain those technical terms to the point that the jury becomes more confused than had the technical terms actually been used during the presentation of the evidence.

Remember, you must show confidence in your case during the opening statement. Indeed, one of the main purposes of the opening statement is to get the confidence of the jury. You should be positive and firm, convince the jury you are acting in good faith, and conclude your opening statement by indicating that the jury should remember four things.

1. To keep an open mind;
2. To wait for the judge's instructions as to the law to be applied and not speculate about the standards they are to use to measure the facts they are hearing;
3. That it is their job to determine where the truth lies, be it on the side of the plaintiff, on the side of the defendant, or at some point in the middle; and
4. That everything you say will be proved.

THE MANNER AND TONE OF YOUR OPENING STATEMENT CAN INCREASE IMPACT

Your opening statement should be delivered in a controlled, soft and conversational tone. Remember, there will be more than enough time during cross-examination and closing arguments to drive points home in a forceful and, where appropriate, emotional tone of voice.

You should establish yourself in your opening statement as the lawyer in control of the case. Excitement during opening statements is typically wasted as the jury hasn't yet heard anything to get excited about.

EFFECTIVE PREPARATION AND PLANNING FOR AN OPENING STATEMENT

You should start to formulate your opening statement almost as soon as you first start to handle the case. Keeping in mind how a judge or jury will look at the case and what you will say to them, you should start either an opening statement file or designate a section of your trial notebook for your opening statement. As various thoughts occur to you, you should jot them down for possible future use.

The opening statement file or section of your trial notebook should be built as the case grows and, as various evidentiary matters are considered during discovery, you should list the points to be argued and emphasized.

Outlining Your Opening Statement

An outline is an absolute must prior to preparation of the opening statement in order to ensure that you do not leave out any important points.

Your outline should contain the following items:

- ☐ Nature of action (e.g., negligence, etc.).
- ☐ Names and identities of parties, including introduction of parties.
- ☐ Statement of facts.
- ☐ Plaintiff's contentions and theory.
- ☐ Defendant's contentions and theory.
- ☐ Names of plaintiff's witnesses and identity.
- ☐ Names of defendant's witnesses and identity.
- ☐ Brief description of witness' occupation as it may relate to the case and gist of witness' testimony.
- ☐ Conclusion.

When Should You Plan to Make Your Opening Statement?

There are several possible times when you may make your opening statement:

- As a plaintiff, your opening statement may be made first.
- As a defendant, your opening statement may be made immediately following the plaintiff.
- As a defendant, your opening statement may be reserved and made after the plaintiff rests, but immediately prior to the presentation of your evidence.
- An opening statement may not be made at all, but you should give long and serious thought before you waive an opening statement. Remember, it's the first opportunity *you* have to address the jury.

Whether you reserve your opening statement is dependent upon your particular case.

Assume you represent a defendant in a highly technical and complex medical malpractice case which you believe will not be presented by the plaintiff in an easy-to-understand and logical fashion. In this circumstance you would have ample justification for reserving an opening statement in order not to provide, through your opening statement, any assistance to the plaintiff in making it easier for the jury to understand the plaintiff's case. There are more than enough opportunities for laying out and previewing your theory of the case to the judge and jury through the cross-examination of the plaintiff's witnesses.

On the other hand, where there is a sharp conflict in the facts to be presented to the jury (e.g., the plaintiff's and defendant's witnesses are presenting totally different versions of the facts), you should not reserve your opening statement. By making it following the plaintiff, you ensure that the jury will have heard your side and will have it in mind while the plaintiff's case is being presented.

If you reserve your opening in this situation, it will be difficult for the jury to relate your particular line of cross-examination, and the points you are able to establish, to your overall theme without having had the benefit of an opening statement by you at the outset of the case.

Effective Use of Demonstrative Aids During Your Opening Statement

A technique for making an opening statement more effective is with the use of visual aids and demonstrative evidence during the opening statement itself. These may fall into several categories including blackboards, exhibits that have been stipulated into evidence prior to trial, maps, charts, or other types of demonstrative aids.

For example, a blackboard can be used to outline the proof or diagram the damages in a case. This is particularly useful in a tort situation where the factual elements of a case are significant or where the damages may relate to loss of support, consortium or love and affection. Another use for a blackboard is to illustrate the concept of preponderance of evidence. Your ability to do this may depend upon whether the judge has either ruled on jury instructions or otherwise ruled on such statements. You should also consider using a chart created to illustrate the theory of the case.

One advantage that charts have over blackboards is that charts can be easily marked and referred to at a later point during the case or, if appropriate, even offered into evidence. Remember, an opening statement and what is included in it is not part of the evidence of the case, unless it is received into evidence at some later part of the trial.

HOW TO MAKE AND MEET OBJECTIONS DURING THE OPENING STATEMENT

On occasion you may be compelled to object to the opening statement being presented by your opponent. Conversely, your opponent might feel the need to object to some portion of your opening statement.

The very first rule to follow when you are making your opening statement and are interrupted by your opponent is to immediately request a bench conference. With a jury nothing can be more damaging than an objection delivered in open court, in the presence and hearing of the jury that is sustained, especially if the judge admonishes you.

Immediately upon hearing the word "objection" from your opponent, you should request permission to approach the bench in order to have the objection resolved. If you anticipate an objection (e.g., you see your opponent begin to stand), you should stop speaking because you will have already lost the jury's attention.

The following is a list of the types of objectionable statements which often occur:

- Comments regarding pretrial settlement efforts.
- Disparaging remarks about opposing counsel, the opposing case or opposing witnesses.
- Appeals to racial, religious, economic, social or political prejudices.
- References to wealth or poverty of litigant or propensity of litigant to be wealthy or impoverished.
- Attempts to arouse self-interest of juror as taxpayer or payer of insurance premiums.
- References to opponent's case as false or fraudulent.
- Irrelevant statements.
- Inflammatory statements.
- An overly detailed factual statement which unduly favors one side.
- A statement of the law that should properly be delivered by the judge.

In order to preserve your objections, you must ensure that the statement and the objection to that statement are recorded. Finally, if the objectionable statement has already been made, request an instruction to the jury by the judge directed at curing the objectionable statement.

TECHNIQUES FOR PRESENTING AN EFFECTIVE OPENING STATEMENT

The following statement is an example of a compilation of techniques that can be effectively integrated into your opening statement in order to better demonstrate to the jury:

1. How an opening statement fits into the trial;
2. What to expect following the opening statements; and
3. That they, as the triers of fact, can look towards you for guidance and assistance during the balance of the presentation.

Remember, an opening statement is the first opportunity that a jury has to evaluate you and your case. Prepare for it by keeping in mind that many jurors make their initial judgments regarding your client based upon you and your presentation during the opening statement.

INTRODUCTION TO OPENING STATEMENT

Ladies and gentlemen of the jury, Your Honor, this is the opening statement. Members of the jury, an opening statement is not unlike a road map. By itself, a road map will get you nowhere. In addition to the map you need a vehicle—a car. The vehicle which will get you to the conclusion of this case is the presentation of evidence which is to follow the opening statements. However, as we know, a road map on a trip serves a very useful purpose itself. It allows a traveler to determine the direction which he or she will take on the trip which is to follow. It allows that traveler to orient him or herself during the trip and to look for certain landmarks in order that he or she does not become lost.

An opening statement is really no different. It allows me to present a road map of the journey on which we are about to embark. It allows me to share that road map with you and to take you on a journey of facts and evidence in order to reach the ultimate destination. The destination of this journey is the conclusion that my client. . . .

Now it's been said in another vein that every public

speaker has three opportunities to address his audience. At the outset, the public speaker will tell you what he will say. Then the public speaker says it and, finally, he tells you what has been said.

And indeed, the opening statement is nothing more than telling you what is about to come. Then we will present the evidence, following which we will talk about what that evidence means.

Now His Honor will, at a later time, instruct you about the law to be applied in this case, but I'd like you to imagine something in your mind, something that perhaps will help you, as it has helped me, to weigh and evaluate the evidence. What I'd like you to imagine is a cardboard box, much like television sets come in or the type of cardboard box you might see at the grocery store.

Now that box is empty. What I'd like you to do is, as the evidence unfolds in the courtroom, as you listen to the witnesses testify, as you see the documents, I want you to collect that evidence in the box. Not only the evidence that is presented by my clients but also the evidence put on by the other side. Listen to that evidence very carefully, but above all else keep an open mind.

Now when this trial is over, I'm going to have another opportunity to address you before you retire for your deliberations. That will be during the closing argument. Now there is a difference between an opening *statement* and a closing *argument*. In this opening statement I will tell you what I intend to prove and what the evidence will indicate and will be. During the closing argument, I will argue what that evidence has proven and the result that you should reach.

During that closing argument, I am going to go back to that box and you and I together are going to take that evidence out piece by piece and examine it. First we'll examine it against what is contended by my adversaries and then we'll examine it and measure it against what is contended by my clients.

Now as I indicated, listen carefully and collect and consider the evidence to be presented to you.

At this point I'd like to describe for you the facts which give rise to this lawsuit. This is a complaint for negligence (or as appropriate).

DISCUSSION OF THE FACTS

Let's now talk about the way in which we will prove these facts. You are going to hear a number of witnesses including (list the names and identities of the witnesses).

DISCUSSION OF THE WITNESS' TESTIMONY, AS WELL AS THE USE OF DEPOSITIONS

Now ladies and gentlemen of the jury, having had this road map drawn and having gotten ready to collect the evidence in our cardboard box, let's embark upon the journey, the actual trial, and let's use the roadmap to reach our destination.

I thank you very much for your attention to this point and am confident that you will pay the same careful attention and consideration to the balance of this case.

A Model Opening Statement for Establishing Control

Let's turn to an actual opening statement made in a negligence case to see how these techniques are actually integrated into a trial setting.

> Your Honor, ladies and gentlemen of the jury, we have now come to that portion of the case . . ., as the Court indicated to you, where I have the opportunity to make my opening statement.
>
> As the Court indicated to you already, what I say is not evidence. It has been said in public speaking that what you are supposed to do is tell the people what you are going to say, then say it, and then tell them what you have said, so you get three shots at it.
>
> I guess in this portion of the case what I am about to do is tell you what evidence we expect to put in; then in the evidentiary portion, following my opening statement, we will put the evidence in, and then at the closing statement I will tell you what the evidence, in our estimation, proved.

Note: The intent of making this analogy was to be able to refer back to it in the closing argument as a means of drawing the whole case together.

> But, as I indicated, this is, more or less, the preview of what you may expect.
>
> I am not going to ask you in any way to forget the evidence you have already heard. We have been here too long to forget anything, but I do want you to bundle it up into a big carton in your minds and move it to one side. I am going to ask you to draw upon it as I put on my client's case.
>
> I think that as the evidence unfolds before you, you are going to relate things—and I will ask you to do this—in your own mind, to reach into that carton and pull something out and match it up against the evidence that we offer, but for now I will ask everybody to wrap it up and put it in that carton and shove it to one side so I can start with a clean slate.

Note: There is no doubt at all but that if the jury had been asked whether or not they visualized a big cardboard carton at this point in the statement, they would have responded in the affirmative. The device of asking the jury or trier of fact to mentally visualize a common object or common experience as a means of assisting them in understanding or organizing difficult or complex facts in an effective technique.

> I will apologize right now, because there will be some repetition. I think, unfortunately, it is the function of the new personality, more or less being the emcee, that there is going to have to be some repetition, basically by way of foundation, so that you can better relate things in your own mind to what has gone on before. There will be little buzz words and things that may help you reach into this section of your mind and recall the prior testimony.
>
> Repetition will be kept down to the absolute, barest minimum. You will not be subjected in any way to a rehash or restatement of evidence that has already gone in.
>
> Now, we have a very, very simple case.

Note: The primary risk in making statements about the simplicity of a party's case rests in the juror's unspoken statement "If it's so simple, why do I have to be here?" To the extent such a risk exists, you may choose to accept it based upon the fact that by the time you are making your opening (where it has been reserved), the jurors may already be confused. By this time, the jury probably believes that the case is complex and you can dispel that notion.

> It is not in any way complex. We will not present it in a complex fashion. We won't present it in a confusing fashion at all. The primary aim of my presentation and the evidence presentation that we are about to make is clarity.
>
> We intend to outline the evidence to you in this preview,

this opening statement, so that you will have some sort of guidepost, some sort of signpost with which to follow this theme or the presentation of the evidence, something that you can use to assimilate it all, tie it together in drawing your conclusions.

Now, nobody likes to say that somebody else, any human being, could make mistakes and that those mistakes would cause a tragic death or series of deaths, that those mistakes might affect, not only the lives of the people involved but thousands of lives.

It affects your lives because you are here, and it affects my life because I am here. I think it is a tragedy that we are all here examining the actions of people and passing judgment on them, yet we must.

Note: This introductory language and the analogy to the "big carton" assists the jury in making the transition from a case against the defendant to a case by the defendant. To further assist the jury and the court in understanding the facts of the case, the jury in this case was even given a road map within the road map of the opening statement.

At this point, a detailed discussion of the facts was undertaken. The case under consideration is an aviation tort case.

Let me tell you what the evidence will show. Let's turn first to the National Weather Service facility. You have heard the name of Mr. Ifopo referred to as a National Weather Service observer.

On the evening of January 30 the evidence will show that Mr. Ifopo detected heavy rain at the airport. You will recall that the National Weather Service facility is on the airport in the vicinity of the terminal building, that he detected this first by actually hearing the rain as we might hear it on a building or a car, and then he also heard the clicks of the triple register record. I think you have already been exposed to what the triple register record is. This is the device that records the rainfall intensity and time of start of the rainfall.

Now, according to the triple register record . . . the heavy rain began at approximately 2335. This heavy rain was detected at the airport at that time.

Upon hearing the heavy rain at his location on the airport, Mr. Ifopo went outside because he knew that heavy rain was or could be associated with a drop in visibility. He adjusted his eyes to the darkness and then he went ahead and took his observation.

When he took his observation, he measured the ceiling, and he will describe to you how he did that, and he measured the visibility, and he will describe to you how he did that.

Following those measurements and that observation, he went back inside the National Weather Service facility and recorded the special weather observation. The last entry made on the recording form was the time at which he completed the last entry of the observation itself and proceeded to transmit it to the air traffic control facility, the CAPIS. . . .

In order to avoid errors in the transmission, the normal procedure that was followed required the observation to be coded into numbers, punched onto a teletype tape and then transmitted to the CAPIS facility.

You will hear testimony from Mr. Bateman and from Mr. Ifopo as to the length of time this entire procedure took.

Now, Mr. Bateman, ladies and gentlemen, will testify here live. He was, in fact, the approach controller that evening. He is the man whose voice you have already heard talking to the aircraft. He is the man who cleared for the approach.

The evidence that will be introduced through Mr. Bateman and other materials will prove that immediately upon hearing the teletype start to receive the information, Mr. Bateman went to obtain this weather information, for he knew there was an aircraft on approach, and he wanted to see what the information was.

The evidence, ladies and gentlemen of the jury, will prove that this information was not received by Mr. Bateman in time to be transmitted to the aircraft. The evidence will indicate that there was no delay in the observation; there was no delay in the transmission; there was no delay in the receipt; it was just a matter of the aircraft happening to be on the approach at a given time and the information happening to be transmitted at the same time.

The evidence will further prove that at no time at all during the approach of Flight 806 did the lights in the National Weather Service facility ever go out, ever fluctuate, or flicker. Further, the evidence will prove that, had there been some sort of power fluctuation, one, it would have been observed; and, two, if it had affected any of the equipment at all, the clocks especially, there would have been an entry in the logs to that effect.

The evidence through Mr. Ifopo alone will prove that there was no such power fluctuation on that evening at the times that are relevant to this litigation.

* * * *

Now, on that evening, Mr. Frank Bateman was on duty as the FAA air traffic controller. You will hear Mr. Bateman testify live. The evidence in this area will prove two things: first, that Mr. Bateman was fully and totally qualified to perform the functions of approach controller that evening and, second, that he completely followed the procedures that were expected of him.

Looking first at the area of transmission of weather information, the evidence will show that Mr. Bateman was not certificated to take weather observations. There was no reason for him to be certified because there was a National Weather Service facility at that airport.

The evidence will show that the weather observations

that Mr. Bateman took related solely to wind velocity and direction, and if you will all recall back to the cockpit voice recorder transcript which you have in your jury books, you will detect several instances of Mr. Bateman transmitting wind direction and velocity to the aircraft.

Now, with respect to other weather observations, the limitations placed upon Mr. Bateman primarily fell into two areas. One, he could transmit weather information received from the National Weather Service facility, and, indeed, that is what he did on the evening of January 30, 1974, and, two, he can transmit weather observations without attaching specific values to them.

Not only did Mr. Bateman transmit the record observations from the National Weather Service facility, but he also transmitted his own observations. He did not put a specific value on them, because he was not authorized to do that.

* * * *

The sum and substance of this area of the testimony through Mr. Bateman will be that he did everything expected of him under the terminal manual.

In this area of the case there will be additional evidence that at no time during the approach of Flight 806 did the lights in the CAPIS facility ever flicker, ever fluctuate or ever go out.

The evidence will prove that what Mr. Bateman thought was a power failure was in fact not a power failure.

* * * *

You will hear testimony that the weather on the night of January 30, 1974, was typical weather for the area. Further, with respect to Mr. Bateman the evidence will show that he received no alarms on the instrument landing system; that had there been some malfunction, some defect, some variation in its operation putting the system outside parameters, outside of tolerances there would have been an alarm, and there was none. Not only were there no alarms on the ILS system itself, but the evidence will show that there were no alarms on any navigational aids that evening.

* * * *

First, let's talk about what the evidence will show about the crew members. You will recall that the pilot in command, the captain of this aircraft, was Leroy Petersen. The evidence will show that Captain Petersen, prior to January 30, 1974, was off flying status for approximately five months and that during that period of time he did no flying at all.

The evidence in this area will prove that in something as technical, something demanding as much precision, something demanding as much repeatability as flying a 247,000 pound aircraft, that any time away from the job at all, especially something in the order of five months, has a derogatory effect upon the precision, upon the skill, upon the reflexes.

Captain Petersen had only been into this airport on one other time prior to January of 1974, and that was in May of 1972. The evidence will demonstrate that Captain Petersen had a consistent history of difficulty in flying precision approaches such as ILS approaches; that this was not a single occurrence, but rather the tragic culmination of a course of conduct, of a course of behavior that had manifested itself throughout this man's career as a pilot.

The second-most experienced man in that cockpit on that evening was Mr. Gaines, but Mr. Gaines wasn't even acting as co-pilot. He was in the observer's seat.

With respect to Mr. Gaines, and it is also true with respect to Mr. Phillips and Mr. Green, the flight engineers, each one of them had consistent problems in their area of individual responsibilities and duties as members of flight crews for Pan American. We are, unfortunately, not looking at a single episode that evening. We are looking at the end of a chain of behavior that had manifested itself throughout the years.

Now, let's turn from the men in that cockpit for a

moment, and I don't ever want you to stop thinking of them as anything other than a crew. The evidence will show that this was a crew, a team, and they were expected to operate in a coordinated manner. Nobody should have given away their responsibility; everybody should have acted as one.

However, turn for a moment to the approach itself. The best evidence in this case, as to what actually occurred on that approach, as to what was done, and what wasn't done, what should have been done, what shouldn't have been done, is, in fact, the statements of the men themselves. We have the cockpit voice recorder. We have the statements of the men. They speak either in the written word or they speak by virtue of omission.

The best evidence of what these men did or didn't do relative to the required procedures is their own statements or failure to make statements.

Let's examine a few of the things that this crew had in the way of information. First, one of the very important things, one of the crucial things for an approach, is weather information. The evidence in this area of the case is going to prove that that crew was in the best position of anybody, either on the ground or any place else in that area, to determine what the weather conditions were, either in which they were then operating or which they might become involved in the further course of their operation.

Why do I say this? I say this because they received record weather observations from the ground, they had weather information from Pan American operations and they had their own physical observations.

The evidence will further prove that this crew had training from Pan American in the area of meteorology, that they were expected to make subjective value judgments as to the weather conditions in which they were operating, based upon their training and upon known weather conditions associated with that area of the world.

The evidence will show that this is not an area that grew up overnight, that this is an area into which Pan American was operating before they had an airport there, so now they had three sources of weather information: their own observations, the controller's observations that were transmitted to them from the National Weather Service, as well as the controller's observations of the wind velocity and direction, and the Pan American Operations' observation.

And finally, the evidence will indicate that they had a uniquely valuable, singular resource that was available to nobody else. They had airborne weather radar. They were the only people who had access to weather radar designed specifically to show the weather into which that aircraft would be operating.

When properly used, it had an irreplaceable value to a crew, especially where there was no ground-based weather radar at all, and especially where it was known that the conditions associated with tropical weather were very changeable.

Now, let's turn from weather for a moment and examine the question of procedures. The evidence in this area will prove that there was an utter disregard of required, expected, and trained-for procedures, that there was a breakdown of the crew concept.

These men did not perform their duties as individuals, nor did they perform their duties or live up to their responsibilities as team members.

* * * *

What happened on the approach? The aircraft reached decision height. They had the field in sight, had the approach lights in sight, had the runway lights in sight; they should have had everything else available to them out there in sight to them as well, including the VASI. There is no evidence that there was any problem in the cockpit or that somebody didn't see something.

Now, if we take the flight procedure requirements, the flight operations manual and the aircraft operating manual, those blue books that have been passed back and forth from witness to counsel, and put them in one hand, and we take the cockpit voice recorder and put it in the other hand, the evidence will clearly show what was and wasn't done.

One, there was no crossover. You will recall that a crossover is the requirement that the first officer, the man not flying the aircraft, have the ILS information portrayed in front of him during the approach. The evidence will prove that one of the very, very important key aspects of flying an airplane is repeatability, that there are two men looking at the same thing.

And what happens when we do not crossover? You do not have the repeatability.

The evidence in this area of the case will indicate that there should have been a crossover at the seven-mile DME, but there wasn't.

The evidence will show that it is not a safe, not an accepted, and not a standard procedure for one man to look across and fly by reference to another man's instruments. It is much like sitting in the passenger seat of a car and telling the police officer who is writing a speeding ticket, that the driver was only going 55 miles an hour. You just can't do it.

What else will the evidence prove about the procedures? There were no callouts. There was no callout of 500 feet. There was no callout of 800 feet. There was no crucial rate of descent callout.

The approach of this aircraft on the glide slope was not stabilized. They did not have a steady rate of descent as they proceeded down this slide in space. They varied their rates of descent, varied their speeds. It was not consistent with what was expected of a professional flight crew. Again, a culmination of years and years of shortcomings in these crew members.

The evidence will show that the rate of descent varied from 600 feet to 1500 feet per minute, but that Pan American procedures required callouts any time rates of descent exceeded 800 feet per minute. There was a "never exceed" rate of descent of 1,000 feet per minute. In the last 17 seconds prior to the impact of this aircraft with the earth, the rate of descent went to something approximating 1500 feet a minute, *and nobody said anything*.

Why didn't they say it? Well, the evidence will show that it wasn't because of a lack of information. They had an instant vertical speed indicator right in front of them. The evidence will prove that the purpose of this instrument is to tell the crew what their rate of descent is at the moment they look at it, so they can watch it unwind; they can watch it go up or go down as they increase or decrease the rate of descent.

They also had two barometric altimeters that show them how far they are above mean sea level. You multiply those two instruments—the instant vertical speed indicator and the barometric altimeter—by four cockpit crew members, one of whom has nothing to do in the observer's seat, and you have to ask yourself why didn't they know?

The evidence will prove that the reason they didn't know is that they weren't paying attention. Tragically, this is consistent with the other things that occurred on that flight.

* * * *

Now, these things, as the evidence will prove, are not random requirements. These aren't things that are just thrown in there for the sake of filling a book up. These are things that directly relate to the safety of this approach, the safety of operation. These are standardized requirements.

The evidence will prove that one of the basic precepts of operation of an aircraft is standardization; that a man is able to get into any airplane, operate into any airport on an instrument landing system approach and do it essentially the same way.

The evidence will show that Pan American pilots, and indeed all pilots, are trained to draw upon their past experience, that they are trained to recognize certain things; that they are trained to react to certain things; that there is a repeatability, that there is a standardization. What that results in is the book of procedures that you have had put before you on various occasions.

The evidence will prove that this crew didn't use it, that there was no standardization, that there was no coordination, that there was a breakdown both individually and collectively of the responsibilities that people had a right to expect from these men.

* * * *

Now, when all the evidence is presented it will become clear that the tragic accident on January 30, 1974, was a combination of circumstances. It was the circumstances of that night, of the weather, of the four men that were on the flight deck of that aircraft.

First, the crew was just not up to the standards expected of professional airmen flying for a flag air carrier like Pan American. The evidence will prove, ladies and gentlemen, that Pan American expected their pilots, their flight crew members, to exceed the minimum standards; that they expected them to have a higher level of competence; that they checked them to a higher level of competence; that the standard was set at a higher level of competence.

The evidence will prove that these men on that night didn't meet those standards or expectations. Further, there was a lack of coordination on the approach. They didn't work together as a team. It broke down. Maybe it was the result of individual weaknesses of the men but, for whatever reason, the team broke down. The crew concept evaporated. The men acted as individuals and their own weaknesses took over.

There was a failure to follow company procedures. The evidence will prove that they were expected and required to follow company procedures. You have heard evidence already, and we will introduce additional evidence, on what has been referred to as a "visual illusion." The evidence will show that this is not an unusual, unique or singular occurrence; that indeed it is associated with most airports to one degree or another and that Pan American pilots were trained on January 30, 1974, to be aware of them, to recognize the conditions that bring them about, to compensate for them, and to not allow them in any way to derogate the safety of the approach. This crew failed on all counts.

Nothing associated with the ILS had anything to do with this accident. It happened in spite of the ILS system being there and functioning properly. Nothing having to do with putting lights on trees had anything to do with this accident.

The evidence in this area will prove that Pan American pilots have never been trained to navigate 707 aircraft to the runway by reference to obstruction lights. The evidence will prove that obstruction lights are random lights, random in the sense that even if they are present at an airport, they are different for each airport. They may or may not be present and they are always different.

The evidence will prove that, to the contrary, Pan American pilots are trained from decision height on to navigate by reference to standardized lighting systems.

The evidence will prove that to use obstruction lights is dangerous and misleading, and that this is especially true where you have known lighting systems, like approach lights, like runway lights, like VASI systems, visual approach light indicating systems.

Now, as I indicated, ladies and gentlemen, the best evidence of what occurred that evening is contained on the cockpit voice recorder. We believe that when weighing the statements, the omissions, and the transmissions on that cockpit voice recorder transcript against the procedures and requirements that are already in evidence, the inescapable conclusion will be that this crew failed to live up to the responsibilities required and expected of them.

Now, I have told you in a broad outline form what the evidence will prove. I have repeatedly said, "The evidence will show this," or "We will prove that," and at least it has occurred to me: How are they going to do this?

Well, we are going to do it in much the same way that the evidence has already been presented, through live witnesses in part, and through deposition summaries in part.

In addition to hearing certain Pan American captains

and other flight crew members by way of deposition summary, you are going to hear from a man who flew for Pan American for 34 years, Captain Charles Bassett, a man who retired from that company approximately three years ago as one of their most senior captains, a man who flew the 707, who flew the 747, who was a check pilot, who flew all over the world for this company.

Captain Bassett will testify that, in his opinion, the sole cause of this tragic accident was the nonperformance, the failure to comply, the failure to act in a standardized manner, the failure to follow the crew concept of the Pan American flight crew.

You are also going to hear, in the area of instrument landing systems, from Dr. Richard McFarland. Dr. McFarland is the world's leading authority on instrument landing systems, a professor of electrical engineering, director of the Avionics Engineering Center at Ohio University, and an air transported rated pilot, the same type of license possessed by commercial airline captains, a man who has training in meteorology, a man who has Ph.D. and Master's degrees in electrical engineering and a man who is going to come here, ladies and gentlemen, and testify that the instrument landing system, as it existed on the night of January 30, 1974, generated a very high quality signal in space, and that, in his opinion, nothing—I will repeat—nothing having anything to do with that instrument landing system was in any way causative of this accident.

Dr. McFarland will offer the opinion that neither the equipment on the ground, the installation of it, the grading of it, the flight checking of it, the maintenance of it, or the operation of it was in any way causative of this accident.

You will also hear, ladies and gentlemen, from Dr. Donald Beran. Dr. Beran is with the Wave Propagation Laboratory at the National Oceanic and Atmospheric Administration, what we used to call the Weather Bureau. Dr. Beran is one of the leading authorities in the world in the area of wind shear research, detection, measurement and prediction.

Dr. Beran will testify that it is impossible to do a mesoscale, a small scale weather analysis, for the approach path of Flight 806, and determine what the weather conditions were on that approach path. He will testify that no reliable estimates of the downdrafts or shear can be made as they existed on that approach path and that any attempt to do so is speculation and guesswork.

This is a man who has devoted his professional life to this very area. Dr. Beran will testify that, using a single rain gauge located at the airport and using a single balloon sounding—you hear it referred to as radiosonde—that it is scientifically impossible to reach any reliable conclusion as to what the weather was at a given time in some remote location.

You will also hear from Mr. James Harris. Mr. Harris is the director of the Visibility Laboratory of the Scripps Institute of Oceanography in San Diego. In recent years, Mr. Harris has devoted his professional efforts to the area of human visibility as it relates to pilot operations—the ability of the human visual system to perceive distances, altitudes and related matters—all related to aviation.

Mr. Harris will testify that the use of random lights—like obstruction lights which are random and non-repeated from facility to facility to facility—in lieu of, or even in combination with known lighting patterns, like approach lights, runway lights, or VASI lights, is a misleading and dangerous practice.

You will also hear testimony, ladies and gentlemen, to the effect that there was no requirement, notwithstanding whether or not they would have been misleading, notwithstanding whether or not it would have been dangerous to use them—there was no requirement in the first place to light trees.

Now, these are just a few of the witnesses you are going to hear. I am not going to attempt to go through them all. Indeed, there aren't that many more.

Now, the Court has already told you of the efforts that

all counsel put in on the deposition summaries and to the extent that I rely on depositions it will be in summary form.

I invite you to listen. I invite you to weigh and evaluate. I am confident that, following this process of evaluation and following a weighing of this evidence, that you will all come to the conclusion that the actions of Mr. Bateman, the CAPIS FAA controller, had nothing to do with causing this accident; that the actions of Mr. Ifopo, the National Weather Service observer had nothing to do with causing this accident; that the actions of the technicians at the airport in charge of maintaining the navigational aids had nothing to do with causing this accident; that the instrument landing system itself had nothing to do with causing this accident and that this accident, this tragic accident, occurred despite the best efforts of these men.

* * * *

I know your attention to the presentation of the evidence will be close and careful.

Thank you very much.

3

Direct Examination That Keeps You in Control and Minimizes the Risks of Your Opponent's Cross-Examination

Table of Contents

3

Direct Examination That Keeps You in Control and Minimizes the Risks of Your Opponent's Cross-Examination

THE PURPOSE OF DIRECT EXAMINATION

The purpose of direct examination is to present your case in a clear and concise fashion that puts you in control—and limits the effectiveness of what your opponent can accomplish on cross-examination. If properly accomplished, these two goals complement one another.

Presenting Your Case

There are two approaches to presenting your case on direct examination. The choice you must make is determined by the nature and the facts of your case. On the one hand you may want to lay out your entire case and hold back nothing except for those areas regarding cross-examination. The advantage of this approach is that it presents to the jury all the evidence against which they can measure your opponent's case.

The task to be accomplished if you are successful in this approach towards direct examination is to persuade the jury of the rightness of your cause. If you are successful in persuading the jury, this then shifts the burden to your opponent, who must change the jurors' minds.

The alternative approach is to present your case in an outline fashion with only enough evidence to sustain minimum burden of proof requirements. Built into such an approach are traps laid for your opponent that are tripped on cross-examination and during your rebuttal. The risk of this approach is that you may not be able to convince the jury of the correctness of your position.

Limiting Your Opponent's Case

The corollary purpose of direct examination is to limit the effectiveness of your opponent's case, and to prevent him from gaining control. This should be done by anticipating and planning for every possible defense or affirmative position presented by your opponent and meeting it in the direct examination of your own witnesses. The advantage to anticipating positions, especially positions in your own case that have inherent weaknesses, is that the position and the inherent weakness is not emphasized by it being raised for the first time on cross-examination.

One of the most difficult decisions that you have to make is to stand up when it comes your turn to cross-examine and say, "No questions." More often than not that statement and the decision it reflects is usually the correct decision. If you can force your opponent to cross-examine, that is usually an indication that you have effectively achieved your purpose on direct examination.

Frequently a decision not to cross-examine is made when the direct examination of a witness has not produced sufficient evidence or facts to persuade you that cross-examination is required in order to correct some mis-impression or explore information which is damaging to your case. By putting on direct examination in a clear and concise fashion from your witnesses, you minimize your opponent's alternatives. As the chapter on cross-examination indicates (Chapter 8), the most effective means of proving *your* case is through the cross-examination of your opponent's witnesses.

EFFECTIVE METHODS OF DIRECT EXAMINATION

Properly structuring a direct examination is far more difficult than cross-examination. Direct examination is best equated to the delivery of prepared lines during a theatrical production. Think back to your own drama experience in high school, or in college, or as a member of an audience at a play, and the various thoughts that ran through your mind regarding the naturalness of the actors, the method of delivery of their lines, the sincerity which they brought to their presentation and their overall ability to "be" the characters they were portraying.

The proper presentation of direct examination raises many of the same considerations. The goal of direct examination is to be able to present carefully prepared evidence in a manner that seems spontaneous, sincere and natural. These two requirements are, to a certain degree, inconsistent with one another unless the participants are able to do so in a manner which is natural, sounds unrehearsed and is persuasive.

Question and Answer Technique Allows You to Control the Direction of Examination

The "question and answer" technique is an effective and simple way of presenting direct testimony, especially where the witness does not possess a presence that permits the giving of a coherent, well-spoken narrative.

In a typical question and answer situation you might expect the direct testimony to proceed as follows:

Question: Were you on the corner of 12th and Main Street at noon on January 12, 1982?

Answer: Yes, I was.

Question: At that time did you see a red automobile approaching from the south intersection?

Answer: Yes, I did.

Question: Would you describe the automobile?

Answer: It was red, and had Virginia license plates. It seemed to be going a lot faster than the other cars in the area.

Question: When you say faster than the other cars in the area would you describe that a little further?

Answer: Yes, it seemed to be going almost twice as fast. So fast, in fact, that I commented to my wife about it.

Obviously, the use of a question and answer technique on direct examination allows you to more effectively control the course of the direct examination. It also eliminates a significant amount of the risk that the witness may go off on his own in answering your questions.

Narrative Technique

The use of the "narrative technique" during direct testimony is an effective style when the witness is well spoken, has a good presence and is knowledgeable in the area of the testimony.

As it is ordinarily used in trial, there is certain preliminary questioning such as name, address, age and identification of the witness in the case, and then a broad question which permits the witness to give a narrative answer or answers.

If the witness has been properly prepared, he will need few clarifying questions following the narrative description. If an important point is omitted by the witness, you should ask him if his memory regarding that particular area of testimony is exhausted. If the witness fails to remember you can probe further by questions and answers, seek to refresh the witness' recollection or if appropriate, use a past recollection recorded approach to the witness' testimony.

For example:

Question: Please state your name.

Answer: Michael Johnson.

Question: What is your address, sir?

Answer: 2412 Maple Avenue, Reston, Virginia.

Question: What is your age, sir?

Answer: I am 29 years old.

Question: Sir, were you standing on the corner of 12th and Maple Avenue on the evening of January 12, 1982, at approximately 4:00 P.M.?

Answer: Yes, I was.

Question: Would you relate to the court and the jury what you saw on that occasion, to the best of your recollection?

Answer: Yes. I was standing on the southwest corner at approximately 4:00 as I've indicated. At about that time, there was some noise off to my right, and I turned around. I don't know whether it was engine noise or the commotion of people, but I did turn around and I saw a red car. A Ford, I think. It looked like a Thunderbird with Virginia plates moving down the street in an erratic fashion towards me. (The witness would then go on and relate the balance of his narrative testimony.)

Control the Narration with the Question and Answer Technique: Following the conclusion of the witness' narrative explanation of his testimony, you can then probe with individual questions. For instance:

Question: Sir, during your testimony you indicated you saw the automobile moving in an "erratic fashion." Would you explain to a greater extent what you mean by erratic?

Answer: Yes. He seemed to be crossing over the centerline and then moving back towards the curb. The car did this a couple of times in the 20 to 30 seconds that I observed it prior to the accident in the intersection.

Forced Question Technique Keeps the Witness on Track

In some situations a witness is unable to give a narrative statement of his testimony without an inordinate amount of guidance by you. Or, you may find yourself confronted with a situation where a judge will not permit the narrative answers to be used because it may be difficult for your opponent to make timely objections.

When faced with this situation, the "forced question" technique may be helpful. In effect, it is a combination of the use of the question and answer technique and the narrative technique in that it uses very short and forceful questions to keep the witness on track.

Examples of the types of questions that might be used in the forced question technique are:

- What was said?
- Who was there?
- Where was it said?
- When was it said?
- How much did he want?
- What color was it?

In effect, the use of these short, forceful questions, interjected by you during the presentation of a narrative, amount to a fence being built around the witness. This helps keep the witness on track.

Because you are basically asking who, what, when, why, where and how questions, a potential objection you might come up against is the fact that the answer to your question is obvious from the context of the testimony. For example, assume that the witness is testifying as follows:

Answer: I then saw the car move off to the left and. . . .

Question: How far to the left?

Answer: Towards . . . towards the curb.

Another potential objection by your opponent is that you are interrupting the witness' answers.

Once again, such an objection can typically be overcome by pointing out that your questions are not leading in nature, but rather meant to be explanatory. Usually this objection will not be successful.

The following example illustrates the use of narrative direct testimony coupled with interjected clarifying questions.

Question: Why don't you just go ahead and tell us sort of a stream of consciousness thing, whatever you remember of those first days in the hospital.

Opposing Counsel: Objection, Your Honor. I think it's an improper question to ask a witness to give a stream of consciousness or narrative on direct examination.

Judge: I will overrule the objection.

Answer: (By the witness) The first thing I remember is being awakened and opening my eyes and seeing my father. I don't remember having any feelings of pain at that moment.

Later—and I can't relate to specific time frames—but at some later point, I became aware that I had tubes up my nose and down my throat and in my arms, and I became vaguely aware of my immediate surroundings with paraphenalia around the bed. My movement being restricted.

Next thing I remember is a nurse coming and shooting something down my throat that made me cough, and that's the first time I became aware of excruciating pain during my stay at the hospital.

Question: Where was the pain located?

Answer: Mainly in my abdomen, and the treatment continued for a period of time, they did that a number of times. Some days after, when I became more aware of the total environment and the ward and the people in the ward I knew that they were concerned with my movements and tried to restrict my movements very much in the bed to keep me flat on my back.

Question: How did they do that?

Answer: I'm not sure, I think it was sandbagging, some restriction that prevented my rolling over and then I became extremely concerned that I wouldn't be able to walk. So I asked them if I couldn't try to stand up and they went and asked whoever was in charge. Two orderlies came back and said yes, they would lift me into a standing position. So they did and I put a little bit of weight on my feet and I had tremendous amount of pain and screamed out and they laid me back down.

Some time later I told my dad that I wanted to return to a hospital in Tulsa. He said he would check on it and see what the doctors had to say about it. So they approved it and my dad made arrangements for an ambulance plane to fly me to Tulsa.

Question: Let's stop right there. What were the areas of your body that were hurting you?

PREPARING WITNESSES FOR DIRECT EXAMINATION IN A WAY THAT ANTICIPATES YOUR OPPONENT'S STRATEGY

It is important when preparing a witness for direct examination that both you and he understand the importance of ensuring that the testimony is presented in the most favorable, advantageous and simple-to-understand fashion. Additionally, preparation for direct examination should also be done in a manner so as to anticipate cross-examination.

The use of a witness briefing checklist is a valuable trial aid that provides assistance in preparing your witnesses to testify. The checklist which follows is one you should use as an outline to be supplemented as needed for your particular case.

Witness Preparation Checklist

☐ Explanation of the Litigation:

- Who's suing whom—interested parties;
- Issues involved—general theories;
- What's at stake—damages sought/reputation/precedent;
- Case—the lawyers/investigators/experts/judge/jury;
- Witness involvement in whole scheme of things:

  - — not being sued personally
  - — no impact on employment
  - — time demands
  - — likelihood of having to come to trial
  - — involvement with other witnesses/experts;
- Explain possibility of settlement.

☐ Background of the Deponent/Witness:

- Connection with litigation;
- Education—special licenses/skills;
- Employment history;
- Exposure to legal system;
- Prior testimonial experience;
- Anxieties concerning upcoming deposition/trial;
- Personal stake in the outcome;
- Prior briefing/prior conversations.

☐ Courtroom/Deposition Procedures:

- Room/courtroom arrangement;
- No informality in courtroom—smoking, coffee breaks;
- No judge in deposition;
- Order of interrogation/description of lawyers;
- Court reporter present/transcript typed/oath;
- Read back capability;
- Witness review and signature (deposition);
- Purpose of testimony as distinguished from deposition—discovery, preservation;
- Demeanor/dress;
- Objectives of opposing lawyers/opponents' methods;
- Use of deposition/impeachment;
- Presence of consultants, observers, etc.;
- Requirement to answer all questions unless instructed not to answer, objection sustained, etc.;
- Objections/legalese;
- Duty to tell truth, not to speculate, volunteer information or render personal opinions;

- Interrogation, not conversation;
- Explain that you may not ask too many questions of your own witness except for clarification in deposition;
- Explain that it will be difficult to give advice during the deposition while on the record; therefore, we suggest some pointers at the pre-deposition conference.

☐ Advice on Conduct During Testimony/Deposition:

- Do not bring notes, books, etc., with you to the courtroom or deposition; if you relied on them in preparing, they can be taken from you and you can be cross-examined about them;
- Tell the truth succinctly;
- Long narrative answers should be avoided if possible unless agreed on in advance;
- The more subjects you bring up, the more questions asked;
- Do not volunteer information, explanations, opinions, rumors;
- Do not try to memorize your answers;
- Listen to questions carefully—if you don't understand, have the lawyer repeat the question;
- Answer the questions asked, not what you suspect he's trying to get at; don't help with his questions; let him earn his fee;
- Treat questions on important matters with caution;
- Ponder the question, consider the interrogator's choice of words (e.g., "Do you always . . ."');
- Watch for buzzwords, e.g., safe, duty, mistake, emergency;
- Is the questioner putting words in your mouth with leading questions? Correct the wording in your answer;
- Is the questioner setting you up, pinning you down or building you up and then showing that you didn't measure up to that image?
- You must pause before answering to:
  - — give yourself time to formulate an honest, short, direct answer
  - — give your lawyer time to analyze the question/answer factually

  - give your lawyer time to analyze the question/answer legally and then object, if appropriate;
- After you have answered, explain or rephrase your answer only to correct an error or obvious misunderstanding;
- Listen to attorney objections for a hint as to what's wrong;
- Beware of a questioner's inquisitive stare, whereby he hopes you will elaborate;
- If interrupted, make sure to go back and finish your answer;
- Avoid a rapid question/answer conversation with the questioner; remember he wants to put you at ease and get you to agree with his version of the facts;
- Remember to answer the question in the appropriate time frame (e.g., procedures at the time of the accident v. current procedures);
- Recollection—if you don't remember say so. If you're not sure, qualify your answer, example:
  - "approximately"
  - "as best as I can recall right now";
- Be careful when explaining distances, time, amounts, speeds, degrees, etc.;
- Exhibits—peruse the entire document:
  - verify its effective date
  - who authored it
  - is it complete
  - don't testify from out-of-date materials
  - is a passage being taken out of context
  - be careful in explaining "why" a document was published
  - maps, photographs, diagrams—if asked to mark, draw large circles, brackets, etc., don't pin yourself down if there is a possibility of inaccuracy;
- Explain that even if a question asks for a "yes" or "no" answer, you may need to explain your answer briefly where qualification is necessary;
- Your profession may require immediate reaction to situations

(e.g., policemen, etc.)—testimony is not such a situation, take your time, find answers in documents if appropriate; if you don't know an answer, say so;

- If asked on cross-examination, readily admit that you had a conference with your attorney and that he advised you to tell the truth, listen carefully, etc.;
- Be courteous, avoid jokes and wisecracks, temper, oneupmanship;
- Be reluctant to express opinions in areas outside your expertise;
- Don't look to your attorney for help in answering;
- Don't discuss the case or your testimony with opposing lawyers or their assistants during breaks and lunch;
- Do not get involved in arguments among attorneys;
- Be careful not to second guess what other people did and why. It's easy to have 20/20 hindsight, but without knowing all the factors surrounding another person's actions, such retroactive analysis is speculative;
- Be careful of hypothetical questions constructed to be analogous to the facts of the case. If not portrayed exactly as you know the situation to be, explain that you can't answer because you don't have enough essential information in the hypothetical to answer it correctly. Be prepared, however, to supply the needed information. If at any time you need a break, tell your attorney;
- Be aware of trick questions (example: Assuming facts that haven't been established, words with double meanings, compound questions);
- Explain that sometimes a lawyer can create a false or incomplete picture by asking only certain questions and that the witness can't always set things straight by himself but must wait until you have a chance to clear up the record on re-direct or cross-examination;
- Be careful of questions such as "are these documents all you

have reviewed?" "have you told me everything you know about. . .?" Qualify your answer in the event you remember something between the deposition and time of trial;

- If asked about embarrassing matters, be forthright and attempt to provide a fair and complete explanation of what happened. (Example: mistakes, previous accidents, failure in school, arrests.) If you hide something and it is discovered, your credibility can be critically impeached.

☐ Factual Review of the Case:

- Explore witness' recollection;
- Explain that the lawyer needs to be educated:
  - — factual/technical information
  - — potential witnesses
  - — documents
  - — statements/notes
  - — rumors;
- What manuals, directives, policies, rules, guidelines, etc., if any, control your actions in this case;
- Explore responsibilities in relation to other witnesses;
- Go over critical details of incident giving rise to lawsuit;
- Advise witness that he needs to brush up on terminology or some aspect of his profession in which he has gotten rusty since the incident(s) giving rise to the lawsuit;
- Be careful about over-educating the witness about matters outside his area of responsibility;
- Avoid revealing specific legal theories to witnesses;
- Explain what you believe to be opposing counsel's version of the facts;
- Review anything your witness prepared, wrote, signed, testified to or had recorded.

☐ Rehearsal:

- Conduct a mock interrogation;
- If a colleague is present, have him make objections;
- Make sure the witness is following the advice you gave him;

- Try out some of the tough questions you anticipate opposing counsel will ask;
- If videotape equipment is available let the witness see himself as he answers questions and is examined;
- Try to trap the witness into admissions;
- Answer any questions the witness has;
- Leave your telephone number with the witness should something come to mind after the conference.

USING EXHIBITS DURING DIRECT EXAMINATION

You should pay careful attention to the actual handling and use of exhibits during all phases of a trial, particularly during direct examination. It is during direct examination of your own witnesses that you must know exactly what exhibits you intend to use. The exhibits should be readily available, in sufficient quantity, to ensure that every appropriate person in the courtroom has a copy.

Prior to the commencement of the trial, either at the pretrial or at some other appropriate time, you should attempt to get stipulations from opposing counsel as to the admissibility of the exhibits. You should also have all of your exhibits pre-marked. Many local rules require that the exhibits be pre-marked so this would be something that need not be voluntarily accomplished by either you or opposing counsel. The practical aspect of having exhibits pre-marked is that far less time is taken in trial fooling with pieces of paper or other types of exhibits while a judge or jury sits by impatiently.

You should have:

- One copy to be marked as an exhibit, usually the original;
- A copy for the witness to use while testifying if not using the original;

- A copy for the judge to refer to if he is not going to utilize the original;
- A copy for the court reporter in the event that there are any quotes or reading to be done from the exhibit;
- A copy for the court clerk and possibly the law clerk; and
- Copies for opposing counsel and yourself.

While this may necessitate a large amount of copying prior to the trial, the benefits pay off during the direct examination when you are in a position to demonstrate to the court the degree of your organization.

How to Handle Documents in the Courtroom

At trial, documents should be handled in the following manner:

Question: There is one more picture that I want to show you, Mrs. James. I request it be marked for identification as plaintiff's exhibit 24-B.

Clerk: Plaintiff's Exhibit 24-B marked for identification and placed before the witness.

Question: Can you identify what has been marked as Exhibit 24-B for identification?

Answer: This is another picture of the house. It could be about January, 1973.

Question: Is that also an accurate representation of the appearance of the house?

Answer: Yes, it is.

Question: And that is a small colored photo, is it not?

Answer: That's right.

Counsel: I offer 24-B for identification into evidence, your Honor.

Opposing Counsel: No objection, your Honor.

Judge: It will be admitted.

Several other procedures should be used in connection with exhibits that are going to be referred to or used on direct examination:

- ☐ Be sure to prepare an exhibit list.
- ☐ Every exhibit should be shown to the witness with whom it will be used in order to give the witness an opportunity to familiarize him or herself with it. The witness should also be asked to explain the exhibit to you if it is an exhibit which the witness is likely to be more familiar with than you are. By doing so, you will be able to ensure that your understanding of what the exhibit is and means does not differ in any way with the witness' understanding.
- ☐ You should ask the witness any questions regarding the exhibit in order to ensure that all possible conflicts are resolved.
- ☐ Each exhibit, including copies, should be placed in an individual folder marked with the exhibit number, identification and, if possible, a summary of the exhibit along with the name of the witness with whom the exhibit will be used.
- ☐ Make arrangements for overhead projectors, blowups of any exhibits which might be needed and, if appropriate, copies of the exhibits that will be repeatedly referred to for inclusion in the trial/jury book. (For a discussion of the trial/jury book, see Chapter 1.)

TECHNIQUES FOR HANDLING SPECIAL SITUATIONS WHILE THE WITNESS IS ON THE STAND

Despite all of the preparation that you might engage in for direct examination, things can go wrong. Human beings are not "programmable." The fact that you expect a witness to say something, the fact that the witness has indicated to you that he will say something, the fact that you are confident that the witness will say something, is frequently not indicative of what the witness will actually say.

There are a number of techniques to be utilized in the event certain things occur while the witness is on the stand.

How to Handle a Witness Who Forgets Vital Information

- Attempt to ask questions around the area of questioning that the witness has forgotten in order to jog or shake his memory.
- If appropriate, refresh the witness' recollection using whatever documents are available. (For a complete discussion of this technique see the next section on refreshing recollection.)
- If appropriate, utilize the technique of prior recollection recorded with a report or statement of the witness made at or about the time of the occurrence which was truthfully prepared in the normal course of events. (For a complete discussion of this technique see the section on past recollection recorded.)

What To Do If a Witness Changes His Story

- Claim surprise and cross-examine.
- Impeach your own witness.

What About a Witness Who Uses Slang or Profanity?

- If the witness uses slang, have him explain the context of the terms. Oftentimes such slang is indicative of technical terms used in industry or business or, alternatively, may be street talk. Usually going back over this type of phraseology with the witness is the simplest way to explain the context of the usage and the testimony to the judge and the jury.

- In the event the witness uses profanity, you should be careful to observe the reaction of the judge and jury. Obviously, if the profanity is integral to the testimony such as the witness repeating something he heard, there is no problem except that you might want to consider alerting the court to what is to be expected in the testimony.

CHECKLISTS FOR REFRESHING PAST RECOLLECTION AND PAST RECOLLECTION RECORDED

Past Recollection Refreshed: How to Jog a Witness' Memory

The use of the technique for refreshing a past recollection must be proceeded by laying a foundation demonstrating that the recollection of the witness needs to be refreshed. You must prepare your witness to answer "at this time" when he or she is asked a "now" question. If the witness simply indicates that this is "all" he or she remembers as opposed to "at this time" or "now," no need has been shown for a refreshing of a past recollection.

There are basically four steps in refreshing a past recollection of witness:

1. The witness' present recollection is exhausted.
2. Something exists which can refresh the witness' present recollection.
3. The item being placed before the witness is that thing.
4. Having read that item, his or her recollection is refreshed.

Having refreshed the witness' recollection, the item used to refresh the witness' recollection is taken away and he may then proceed to testify from his refreshed recollection.

For example:

Question: What color was the automobile that struck Mrs. Jones, the plaintiff, sir?

Answer: At this time I don't remember.

Question: Sir, do you recall giving a statement a short time after this accident?

Answer: Yes, I do.

Question: Sir, I hand you what has been marked for identification as exhibit 3 and ask you take a moment to look it over. (Witness does so.)

Question: Is that the statement?

Answer: Yes, it is.

Question: And when is it dated, sir?

Answer: Two days after this accident.

Question: Does reviewing that statement refresh your recollection as to what color the automobile was?

Answer: Yes it does.
(Counsel takes statement from witness.)

Question: Sir, having had your recollection refreshed can you now tell us what color the automobile was that struck the plaintiff?

Answer: Yes sir, it was a red automobile.

It should be noted that the refreshed recollection of the witness is what is presented to the court and not what is in the document itself. Thus, the item used to refresh the recollection is not offered into evidence. This is distinguished from past recollection recorded.

It is irrelevant whether or not the item which refreshes the witness' recollection is itself admissible, because the witness is testifying from his or her own recollection refreshed and not from the document. Remember, the essential thing is that the document or item refreshes the witness' recollection, i.e., it jogs the witness' memory. Indeed you can refresh a witness' recollection with anything—newspapers, magazines, books, statements, etc.

The item which refreshes the witness' recollection is not usually read aloud by the witness but must be surrendered before the witness testifies from the refreshed recollection and may not be admitted into evidence itself. However, under some rules of procedure, an item that is used to refresh a witness' past recollection may be admissible for use as impeachment or if the opposing party seeks its admission.

Another Technique For Jogging a Witness' Memory: Past Recollection Recorded

In the event a witness does not have his or her recollection refreshed after reading a document, the technique of "past recollection recorded" is the next step to be utilized. Having established, through appropriate questioning, that the witness' recollection has not been refreshed, you may then go ahead and proceed to introduce the evidence through the device of "past recollection recorded."

In order to do so, you must introduce certain elements of proof. They are:

- The witness' recollection is not refreshed after reading the document.
- The document or writing was made at a time near to the event when his or her memory was fresh.
- If the witness prepared the document, then he or she remembers correctly recording the facts. Alternatively, the witness habitually records certain matters correctly in the normal course of events.

- If someone else prepared the document or report, that the witness read it while his or her memory was still fresh and knew it to be true and correct at that time.
- That the document is in its unaltered original form or, alternatively, is a true copy of the unaltered original.

The following examples illustrate the procedure to be followed in court:

Exhausting Present Recollection:

Question: I hand you what has been marked as Exhibit number 4 for identification. Will you please read it?

Answer: I have done so.

Question: Having read that exhibit, do you have any independent recollection of the events related in that document?

Answer: No.

Question: Does having read that document refresh your recollection?

Answer: No.

The Time of Making the Document:

Question: Can you tell us what that document is?

Answer: Yes. It was a statement prepared by me in longhand and then typed by a secretary who returned it to me for review. Then I signed it.

Question: When did that occur?

Answer: January 12, 198X.

Question: How long was that after the accident?

Answer: That was the next day.

If the Witness Wrote or Prepared the Document:

Question: How can you tell that what has been marked as Exhibit 4 for identification was prepared by you?

Answer: It's in my handwriting (or "I signed it").

Question: What was the occasion of your preparing that statement?

Answer: I was asked to prepare it by a police officer the day after the accident.

Question: Is that statement a correct record of the facts as you knew them to be at the time you prepared the statement?

Answer: Yes it is.

If Someone Else Prepared the Document/Statement Other than the Witness then Testifying:

Question: Can you identify what has been marked as Exhibit 4 for identification?

Answer: Yes.

Question: How?

Answer: I know the individual who prepared this statement and he showed it to me after he had signed it.

Question: When did you first see it?

Answer: I saw it on the date it was prepared.

Question: Did you have occasion at that time to read that statement through?

Answer: Yes I did.

Question: How long after the accident was that?

Answer: The day after.

Question: At that time did you have a clear recollection of the accident?

Answer: Yes I did.

Question: Is Exhibit 4 for identification true and correct to the best of your knowledge?

Answer: Yes.

Verifying the Authenticity of the Document:

Question: Has Exhibit 4 for identification been changed or altered in any way since you read it/wrote it/it was prepared?

Answer: No sir.

Question: Is the statement which you have identified as Exhibit 4 for identification true and correct today to the best of your knowledge?

Answer: Yes.

Admission into Evidence:

Question: Please read the document to the court and the jury.

At this point the document is read by the witness. Typically the document itself is not admissible into evidence at this point but may be moved into evidence by your opponent.

EFFECTIVELY MAKING AND MEETING OBJECTIONS: HOW TO CONTROL THE FLOW OF EVIDENCE

To define and contour the parameters of evidence, there are a number of objections which both you and your opponent have available. The manner in which you use your objections while your opponent is examining his witnesses on direct examination is a key factor in determining the extent of control you have over the development of evidence.

The ability to properly object in court is as much a matter of instinct as knowledge. Notwithstanding all of the aids available in the legal marketplace telling you how to make or respond to objections, experience is the best teacher. As you sit in the courtroom and listen to your opponent's case on direct examination, you will instinctively know when something objectionable is about to be asked, has been asked or will be asked.

It is this instinct which is your greatest asset in controlling the flow of evidence. Not only are you able to limit the nature of the questions, but by carefully crafted objections, you are able to shape the testimony of not only your own witnesses on cross-examination, but your opponent's witnesses while they are testifying on direct examination.

How Can You Make Your Objections Most Effective?

The way you make your objection is as important as the objection itself. Assume your opponent is conducting the direct examination of his key witness. You are preparing to make an objection to a question that has been half-asked and is presently being completed. In order to effectively object, you should stand up and loudly state "Objection, Your Honor." It is imperative that your objection be loudly stated in order to prevent the witness from giving any sort of answer. This is particularly important if the question calls for a yes or no answer.

Prior to trial you should also determine from the judge's courtroom clerk, law clerk or court reporter whether or not the judge wants you to state the basis of the objection such as "Objection, Your Honor, the question is compound and complex."

Following your objection, the court may turn to your opponent and seek a response or, alternatively, ask you for further explanation of the objection. In any event, you have succeeded in breaking the train of thought of your opponent, in bringing a line of objectionable testimony to the court's attention and disrupting the witness' flow of direct testimony.

The corollary to the foregoing is being able to minimize the effectiveness of your opponent's objections when you are conducting direct examination. While you are not able to prevent your opponent from objecting, you can prevent your opponent from getting any additional benefit from an objection other than preventing objectionable testimony from coming into the record.

The way to do this is to, immediately, upon an objection being made by your opponent, state to the court "Your Honor, may we approach the bench?" By going to the bench, the resolution of an objection is made out of hearing of the jury or the witness thereby preventing them from being influenced by any statement which accompanies your opponent's objection. In the event your opponent's objection is sustained, you should return to the questioning and shape it in such a way so as to minimize the impact of the objection to your question.

If the objection is overruled, you should return to your questioning by asking that the question to which there had been an objection be re-read by the court reporter. You should not attempt to re-state or re-phrase the question because the odds are that you will be unable to do so in exactly the way you previously asked it. By asking that it be re-read by the court reporter, you ensure that there cannot be any objection to the question and you emphasize to the jury the fact that the objection was overruled.

A Shopping List of Objections

1. "Objection, Your Honor, the question is ambiguous and unintelligible." This means that either you or the witness cannot figure out what the question means. Obviously, it is imperative that the question not be susceptible of two interpretations or be unduly confusing because the answer may be improperly given.
2. "Objection, Your Honor, the question is compound." This objection is directed at a question which is essentially two questions. Thus, a witness attempting to give an answer to the question may inadvertently give an incorrect answer to the second part of the question or, alternatively, may be giving confusing answers if attempting to answer both parts of the question. For example, "Isn't it true, sir, that you saw the automobile strike the plaintiff and that the automobile was moving very quickly?"
3. "Objection, Your Honor, the question is (vague) (general) (ambiguous) (calls for a narrative response)." This type of questioning calls for a narrative and permits virtually any type of direct testimony to come in response to the question thereby depriving you of the ability to object effectively. For example, "On the day of the accident, what happened?" or "What happened next?"
4. "Objection, Your Honor, the question has been asked and answered already." Obviously, this is an objection which is aimed at stopping an endless direct examination that is repeating the same material. While most courts will permit a certain amount of repetition, the "asked and answered" objection can typically be successful when your opponent has asked the same question more than two or three times.
5. "Objection, Your Honor, counsel is misquoting (or mischarac-

terizing) the testimony of this witness." This is a trial objection that you can use quite effectively to prevent your opponent from shaping the testimony from his or her witnesses by misstating it in a way that is more favorable to the case.

Frequently, such questioning is prefaced by the statement of counsel "So what you're saying . . .," "You earlier testified . . ." or "We earlier had testimony from Mr. Smith that . . ."

An alternative approach to objecting to this technique is to on cross-examination take the proper testimony that had been offered by the previous witness, reconstruct the hypothetical and, hopefully, elicit an opinion that is based upon the actual testimony.

6. "Objection, Your Honor, the document speaks for itself." Obviously, this is an objection that is well-founded, inasmuch as it is directed at the opponent who attempts to characterize from an exhibit in evidence, read passages out of context from an exhibit, or summarize from an exhibit when phrasing a question. Since the exhibit itself is in evidence, the basis for the objection is that the jury is able to read the exhibit and determine exactly what the exhibit says without the need for characterization or summarization by your opponent.

   This objection is not always successful as the following exchange regarding tax returns indicates.

Question: All right, what were your wages in 1971, 1972 and 1973?

Counsel: I object, Your Honor. What's on the tax returns speaks for itself.

Judge: I'm sure that's right, but isn't he just reading from the tax return?

Counsel: That's exactly the point, Your Honor.

Judge: You can cross-examine, I will overrule the objection.

7. "Objection, Your Honor, the question is leading." Leading questions are generally not permitted on direct examination. An exception to this general rule is in the area of preliminary questioning where leading questions will usually be tolerated in order to expedite the presentation of preliminary type evidence (i.e., name, age, date of birth, occupation, basic background facts, etc.).

   Leading questions may also be used on direct examination when a foundation is being laid and the use of leading questions would save time. For example, "Sir, on the date of the accident you were present on the corner of 10th and Pennsylvania Avenues. Isn't that correct?"

   The typical way that a leading question is phrased is "Isn't it true that. . ." or "Isn't it incorrect that. . ." Alternatively, the question may conclude with ". . . isn't that correct?" No matter how the question is phrased the fact that it suggests an answer makes it leading and objectionable. Your objection should be immediately and forcefully made to the use of leading questions because this technique prevents the witness from testifying and substitutes counsel's testimony for that of the witness.
8. "Objection, Your Honor, counsel is arguing with the witness." While this is typically an objection that is made on cross-examination when your opponent is arguing with or badgering your witness, it is also an objection that can be utilized during your opponent's direct examination of his own witnesses in order to prevent counsel from testifying. For example, "And so then, based on your involvement, it couldn't have happened the way that Mr. Smith (your witness) contends, could it?"
9. "Objection, Your Honor, the question assumes facts not in evidence." This is the type of objection that you can frequently make where your opponent is constructing a hypothetical example and building into it facts that are not yet in evidence.

   With non-expert witnesses, such a question frequently starts out with "Do you know . . ." or "Are you aware of the fact . . ." The problem with such questions is that no matter what the witness' answer, your opponent has testified to facts that are not otherwise in evidence. If the witness indicates a lack of knowledge or lack of awareness, your opponent has implied that such is the fact in any case. In such a circumstance you should be quick to object in order to prevent your opponent from testifying and thereby introducing into the record evidence that is not otherwise admissible.

10. "Objection, Your Honor, that question calls for speculation by the witness." Obviously, this objection is directed at questioning by your opponent which seeks to elicit a guess from the witness. For example, "How much do you think it would cost?" or "What's your best guess?"
11. "Objection, Your Honor, the evidence is irrelevant." As a general rule, all relevant evidence is admissible and all irrelevant evidence is inadmissible. However, the judge may exercise his discretion and exclude relevant evidence where it is likely to prejudice, confuse or waste the time of the court.

    There is no black and white as to what is relevant or irrelevant. This is a determination which you must make on the facts of your particular case. However, with any relevancy objection, you should carefully formulate the particular basis for the objection and be prepared to back up the statement that something is irrelevant.
12. "Objection, Your Honor, the witness is incompetent to testify in this matter." As a general rule, every person is competent to testify as a witness unless the law of the state in which you are trying your case provides otherwise (e.g., minors, insane persons, etc.). This is a judgment which must be drawn with respect to each individual case and witness.
13. "Objection, Your Honor, calls for hearsay by the witness." The hearsay objection is probably one of the most frequently used and abused objections that you will run into at trial. As a general matter, hearsay is an out of court statement which is introduced to prove the truth of the matter asserted. However, as we all know, there are a number of exceptions to the hearsay rule under

which evidence that might otherwise be hearsay is still admissible. Accordingly, before objecting to what appears to be hearsay, you should thoroughly understand the exceptions to the hearsay rule in order to ensure that: (1) the testimony that you are objecting to is indeed hearsay; and (2) that it does not fall within one of the hearsay exceptions.

14. "Objection, Your Honor, there is insufficient foundation for this line of questioning." Generally speaking, most evidence mandates that certain preliminary facts or foundations be proved before it is built upon with additional facts or evidence. Thus, for instance, a witness prior to testifying about what the weather was in a certain city, must establish that he was in fact in that city at the time in question or has some other means of knowing the weather. For example:

    Question: Would you please tell us if you can, the extent to which Mr. Vesey's energies and skills went into the development of the Hope Ranch Realty and Investment Company. Do you know anything about that?

    Counsel: Objection, your Honor.

    Judge: The ground, counsel?

    Counsel: The ground that there is no foundation laid.

    Judge: I agree. Lay some foundation.

    In some instances, the court will permit the evidence to be received based upon the promise that it will be tied up through a later offer of evidence. If this is the case, you should be sure to move to strike the prior testimony and evidence if it is not connected up.

15. "Objection, Your Honor, this evidence is cumulative." The "cumulative" objection is to be distinguished from the "asked and answered" objection, in that an objection based on cumula-

tiveness pertains to the submission of evidence to prove exactly the same thing as has already been proven. In many instances, you may find the judge raising this objection himself. This objection is frequently appropriate involving experts. Many attorneys seem to think that quantity outweighs quality and that by parading a large number of witnesses before the jury, the jury will somehow perceive that it is a war of numbers.

16. "Objection, Your Honor, this is not the best evidence." As a general rule, the contents of a writing must be proved by the original document and not by secondary evidence, such as a copy of the document or testimony as to its contents.

    The most significant use of the "best evidence" objection that you may encounter involves the use of summaries where there are voluminous records such as medical records, maintenance records, etc. In such a case, be especially alert to your opponent examining a witness regarding what is contained within certain documents by using summaries through the guise of voluminous writings, thereby depriving you of specific objections that may be available if the documents themselves were used.

    For example, there may be hearsay statements contained within certain records that would otherwise be objectionable, but because the witness is using summaries, you are deprived of the ability to object or control the scope of examination.

How to Decide Whether or Not to Make an Objection

As with most judgments that you'll be making during trial, there is a risk/return analysis that you are going to go through in order to determine whether or not to make an objection. Your goal in making this judgment is to maximize the benefits of objecting while minimizing the risks. In doing this, there are several things you should consider in deciding whether or not to object.

Reasons for Not Objecting During Direct Examination:

- Objections run the danger of alienating the jury and/or the judge. If you make a large number of objections, no matter how well justified, you disrupt the flow of the trial and it appears as if that is the reason you are objecting.
- Objections have the potential for highlighting evidence which is harmful to your case. Throughout the trial you must make certain judgments as to whether or not certain evidence should be explored by way of cross-examination or otherwise. Inherent within this judgment is the effect that the evidence or testimony is having upon the jury. For example, if an especially damaging piece of evidence is coming into the record, yet you are satisfied by your assessment of the atmosphere in the courtroom and the appearance of the jury, that the jury has either not been paying attention or does not understand the significance of that evidence, by objecting you will simply be drawing attention to the evidence and otherwise alerting them that something of significance is occurring. Obviously, this is a calculated risk but one which you must make based upon the best available information at the time.
- Objections to evidence that is otherwise objectionable, but is innocuous. Even though a witness may be rambling, cumulative, going over ground that has already been asked, etc., you might make the tactical decision that it is better not to object in light of the fact that the jury may discount all of the witness' testimony. Of course, there comes a time at which the jury will be looking to you for some relief and, if you successfully object, the jury will be grateful.

Reasons for Objecting During Your Opponent's Direct Examination:

- Excluding improper evidence. This is self-explanatory.
- Preserve issues for possible appeal. Remember, unless you state an objection on the record, you will not have preserved an issue

on appeal. Thus, even though there may be certain factors mitigating against an objection, unless you are confident that your tactical decision is right, you may want to make an objection in a low-key fashion in order to preserve your record on appeal.

- Expose your opponent's unfair tactics or approach. An objection made where your opponent is attempting to testify, to mischaracterize his own witness' testimony, to assume facts not in evidence, etc., can be extremely successful because it will control further tendencies of your opponent, cut-off the pursuit of those tactics at that time and, finally, warn the witness through your objection not to be baited by these approaches.
- Harass your opponent, and keep him off balance. Perhaps the single largest benefit that accompanies every objection, for whatever other valid reason it may be made, is to rattle your opponent, thereby causing him to lose a train of thought. This can be especially effective if your risk/benefit analysis requires you to make an objection at a time when your opponent is starting upon a line of inquiry that will be especially damaging to your case.

  A properly timed and executed objection under these circumstances can have the added effect of damaging your opponent's case by throwing him off stride.

  Obviously, if you are going to object for the purpose of harassing or rattling your opponent, you must do it very carefully and in an extremely controlled and low-key fashion.

Preparing for Objections in a Manner That Maximizes Their Effectiveness

The most effective way to prepare to make objections as you sit and listen to the direct testimony coming from your opponent's witness is to start prior to trial and anticipate lines of questioning and evidence to be developed through various witnesses. By doing so, you will be prepared, before the witnesses start to testify in objectionable areas, to cut them off by an appropriate and timely objection.

Remember, timely and well-placed objections can define the limits of the evidence that can be presented by your opponent. In this regard, where you are dealing with a legal objection that is well founded in the case law or, alternatively, a factual objection that is premised upon the peculiar facts of your case, proper preparation will also permit you to either have available as part of your objection appropriate case citations or, where desirable, a brief on the matter to hand to the court. Typically, this will catch your opponent completely off guard and result in a limitation of the evidence to be received. This would be done out of the presence of the jury in order for the court to be able to give an evidentiary ruling. The manner in which you would seek this ruling is by requesting, through the court, that your opponent make an offer of proof as to a certain line of testimony or evidence. Following the offer of proof, you are able to argue your objection and obtain a ruling.

The motion *in limine* accomplishes the same result of limiting the proof, however it does so on your motion. Procedurally, you would file a written motion *in limine* seeking to preclude the introduction of certain evidence at trial. This could be done at any time prior to trial, at pre-trial, or, if appropriate, at the trial itself. Your opponent will then be required to respond in what amounts to an offer of proof.

HOW THE RIGHT COURTROOM PRESENCE HELPS YOUR CASE

Your Attire Can Project an Image of Control

Little more can be said about suitable dress for the courtroom other than the fact that it should project an image of you as a lawyer in command and control. A number of specialists in the areas of psychology and fashion have commented upon what lawyers should or shouldn't wear. Depending upon the amount of credibility that you attach to such conclusions you, assuming you are a man, should probably wear grey or blue suits, with white shirts, small patterned conservative ties and black shoes. Assuming you are a female trial lawyer, you should be wearing tailored suits and conservative shoes.

At least one study has been done by a litigation consulting firm which revealed that the color of a lawyer's suit does not significantly affect jurors' perceptions about the lawyer. Indeed, while some people suggest that attorneys should wear grey or blue suits, one survey found that brown suits ranked highest when taking into consideration the aspect of power, sincerity and competence as conveyed by the color of a lawyer's suit. None of the jurors in this study were affected by the ostensible client of the lawyer even when they were variously told that the same lawyer was representing either the federal government, or a large corporation.

Thus it would seem that, while there is no rule regarding the manner in which an attorney should dress, good common sense is the best guideline to follow. Avoid flashy clothes. Avoid sport clothes. Avoid anything that would detract from your case and the facts you are to present and that would focus the jury's attention on a particular characteristic of your dress and not your presentation.

Some guidelines to keep in mind in order to successfully convey the proper image to the jury are:

- Jurors have certain expectations that have been fashioned by television as to what a trial lawyer should look like. You are, in many ways, an actor playing a part and should do everything within reason not to disappoint your audience—the jury.
- Don't wear anything—clothes, shoes, accessories, hairstyles, jewelry—which will detract from you. Whatever you wear should have the effect of enhancing your presence in the courtroom and not detracting from it.
- Don't wear the same clothes day after day in the courtroom.

Jurors will fixate on your clothes and realize you are wearing the same clothes. By the same token, don't turn your appearance at the trial into a fashion show with the jury guessing what you'll be wearing tomorrow.

- Don't be a fashion trend setter in the courtroom.
- Don't wear a sweater in the courtroom. It conveys a sense of casualness.
- Whether you're a man or a woman, don't take your suit jacket off in the courtroom.
- Remember, you want to dress in such a way so as to convey a sense of power and control in the courtroom.

Your Decorum Impresses the Judge and Jury

The proper decorum that you as a trial lawyer should have in a courtroom is one that is governed by the very place in which you are practicing your profession. A courtroom, be it state, federal or local, is a place which dispenses justice and juries view the judge as the symbol of justice. Thus, they expect that you, as an attorney, will respect the judge and act accordingly.

There are a number of things which you must observe, be it as part of direct examination or otherwise:

- Always rise when addressing the judge.
- Always be polite when addressing the judge.
- Always address the judge as "Your Honor."
- Juries resent rudeness, but there is absolutely nothing wrong with being firm but polite. Being polite, however, does not mean knuckling under. Circumstances will always occur when you find yourself stating "With all due respect, Your Honor, I disagree with the Court's conclusion and. . . ."
- Always address your objections to the judge and not to your opposing counsel.

- Do not directly address the jury but stand back from the jury box as well as the witness stand unless you request and are granted permission to proceed.
- At all times you should appear calm, cool and, most importantly, in control of the situation.

Part of respecting the court and the court's position, and conveying that respect, is requesting permission of the court to:

- Proceed with voir dire;
- Question a witness;
- Approach a witness or the jury box;
- Approach the bench;
- Have the witness leave the witness stand to approach a chart or give a demonstration;
- Have the marshal or the court clerk get a witness;
- Have the clerk mark an exhibit or hand an exhibit to the judge or witness.

Just as there are certain things which you should do, there are certain things which you should not do:

- Do not walk around while questioning your witness on direct examination. This will distract the jurors and the judge and cause the focus of attention to shift from the evidence to you.
- Do not hold notes. If you must use notes, something which is entirely proper, have your notes on a nearby podium if you are standing behind or near one.
- Do not lean or slouch.
- Never show surprise and, conversely, never show anger.
- Never turn your back on the judge. Your role as a lawyer is, in many ways, like an actor in a play. One of the cardinal rules of theatrics is to never turn your back on your audience.
- Develop a technique by visiting the courtroom beforehand and

familiarizing yourself with the lines of sight and angles that will permit you to remain facing the judge and the jury and yet move around the courtroom freely to accomplish what needs to be accomplished.

- Never, under any circumstances, show disrespect for the court or the judicial process in the courtroom, in the hallways of the court house, or during the recess. While we have all had bad experiences with the courts on occasion, they are occupational hazards and should be kept in our offices.

Establish a Record That Conveys the Essence of Your Case

You should remember at all times that while you are presenting your case a court reporter is taking down everything, stenographically. Oftentimes after examining a witness either at trial or deposition you will return to your office with a glow of satisfaction over the total devastation that you have brought to bear upon the witness during your cross-examination. A few days or weeks later when the written transcript arrives, you find that it doesn't read quite so well. Sentences are choppy, you weren't clear in your questioning, you didn't properly handle or identify exhibits during the examination, and it is just generally flat. The record just doesn't speak.

Since it is difficult to inject emotion into written words, you must be very careful to establish a record that conveys to those who are reading it, be it the trial judge or the appeal judge, the essence of your case. The record is, by its very nature, "cold" in that it lacks the emotions that are present in the courtroom.

In order to establish a record that will give your client the best possible chance of prevailing, you should:

- Make your exhibits speak. Always refer to them by number giving a full description. For example, "Sir, I ask the court clerk to place in front of you what has been marked as plaintiff's exhibit number 12, a letter dated ________ from ____________ to ____________."

- Make sure distances are in the record, as opposed to explanations indicating "about this big." The proper way to ensure that the record is clear when a witness testifies in such a fashion is for you to state something along the following lines: "The record should indicate that the witness is holding his hands approximately eight inches apart. Sir (referring to the witness), is that approximately accurate?"
- Have documentary evidence clearly marked and received into evidence. Frequently, you are so wrapped up in the trial itself that you might forget to ensure that documentary evidence you utilized on direct examination is marked and received into evidence. You should be sure that all of the exhibits used by your witness on direct examination have been marked for identification, offered and received into evidence in order to ensure completeness of the record.
- Make sure that the witness clearly marks points on diagrams, pictures or maps. Typically it is a good idea not to have a witness use an X or a pencil point size dot to mark such locations, but rather to utilize a circle indicating a general location. In order to ensure that the record accurately reflects what has been done, you should insert language along the following lines: "Sir, I ask you to draw a circle around the position on the map to which you have just testified. Having done that please put your initials next to that circle along with today's date."

The reverse, the ways *not* to create an effective record, should be quite obvious. During direct examination you should avoid the use of pronouns such as "this," "it," and the use of the term "etc." Remember when you are speaking in court you must avoid vague references or ambiguities that in normal conversational circles might be perfectly acceptable. At all times you should be precise and confident in your approach, conveying to the jury your control of the situation and a sense of ease in the courtroom.

4

How To Make Dramatic Use of Demonstrative Evidence

Table of Contents

4

How To Make Dramatic Use of Demonstrative Evidence

HOW TO MAKE EFFECTIVE USE OF CHARTS AND DIAGRAMS

The simplest and most basic forms of demonstrative evidence are charts and diagrams. Every time you set foot in a courtroom, you have access to a chalkboard or large pad. It is common practice to permit the introduction of evidence through the use of charts and diagrams where the facts of the case cannot be easily or clearly described without illustration.

Tort litigation, which typically involves a great many facts, is particularly suitable for such devices. Of course, as with all types of evidence, there must be a proper foundation laid even when the purpose is to simplify the evidence.

As a general rule, I don't recommend the use of a blackboard. You should utilize a large artist's pad or, if a blackboard must be used, you should arrange to have photographs taken of diagrams or other material before they are replaced or erased.

Graphic Testimony Can Be a Valuable Aid to You and the Jury

In addition to using charts and diagrams in connection with explaining factual patterns, you should consider using diagrams or charts made while examining witnesses. Such diagrams or charts would be graphic representations of the witness' testimony.

In a typical trial setting, the jury will listen to the verbal testimony, review the documentary exhibits or demonstrative evidence and retire to reach a verdict. Sometimes the judge will let them have some of the actual evidence in the jury room with them—sometimes not. On occasion, the judge may permit certain testimony to be re-read to the jury. In virtually no circumstance will the jury be given the entire trial transcript, even assuming its availability.

Considering this, the technique of preparing a witness' testimony in graphic form and then having it received into evidence is extremely beneficial. Not only are you able to have a tangible record of the testimony presented before the jury, but you may also use it with other witnesses and during your closing argument.

Producing and Using Charts and Diagrams: A Demonstrative Evidence Kit

When using charts or diagrams you should keep color and size in mind. There should be sufficient contrast to allow the charts to be seen by the jury. They should also be large enough so that the jury can focus its attention on the chart. You should also consider having 8½″ x 11″ copies of any large chart available in order that they may be easily included in any trial record or record on appeal. Smaller copies are also convenient because they can be easily referred to by the judge and jury during the trial.

When using charts and diagrams you should assemble what can be loosely called a *demonstrative evidence kit*. In effect, this is nothing more than a collection of aids, both documentary and demonstrative, that will be of assistance to you in the courtroom.

The following items should be included in your demonstrative evidence kit:

- ☐ An assortment of felt tip markers, both narrow and broad tip, in various colors. Included within these should also be day-glo colors that can be used for high visibility in the courtroom.
- ☐ An assortment of colored grease pencils that can be used to write on celluloid overlays.
- ☐ An 8′ to 12′ metal tape measure and a six-inch ruler.
- ☐ A set of calipers that can be utilized to take precise measurements.
- ☐ Two small stainless steel telescoping pointers. These are similar to automobile radio antennas and are about the size of ballpoint pens when folded up.
- ☐ A small stapler with spare staples.
- ☐ Preprinted evidence stickers.
- ☐ Thumbtacks, preferably those with the large plastic heads on them that can be easily removed and handled in a courtroom.
- ☐ A selection of white and colored chalk.
- ☐ Paper clips.
- ☐ A number of large bulldog type clips that can be used to affix charts or diagrams in the courtroom.
- ☐ A small calculator.
- ☐ Metric conversion tables.
- ☐ Extension cords for use with slide projectors, opaque projectors and similar equipment.
- ☐ Blank self-stick white labels.

The whole idea of having these types of things available—and the list can go on—is to not be caught short in the courtroom. In order to present your ideas effectively, be sure to plan before you enter the courtroom for special aids you may need.

A Sampling of Ideas

The following are some examples of charts and diagrams that have been utilized in actual cases to demonstrate specific evidentiary points.

A Step-by-Step Introduction of Physical Evidence: As the victim was returning to his Northwest Washington, D.C., home one January evening, he was confronted by two unknown subjects when he got out of his car. The victim was robbed of various personal items and was shot once in the thigh and once in the left side damaging a major vein. He lay in a critical condition following surgery but eventually recovered after a lengthy stay in the hospital. The two unknown subjects were identified along with the driver of the getaway car.

A chart was prepared for the trial to familiarize the court with the crime scene layout and to illustrate a step-by-step introduction of the physical evidence. A chart approximately four feet in size was made with a magnetic base and magnetic symbols were prepared for attaching, as needed, to mark the locations where each bit of evidence was discovered. See Figure 4-1.

Two of the defendants drew jail sentences and the third, who was the driver of the getaway car, was granted immunity for his cooperation in bringing the case to a close.

Explanation of Complex Cases: In 1979, a case was brought to trial in the Washington, D.C., area detailing charges of a massive conspiracy to bribe public officials to obtain Government contracts and to fraudulently secure money from these contracts and

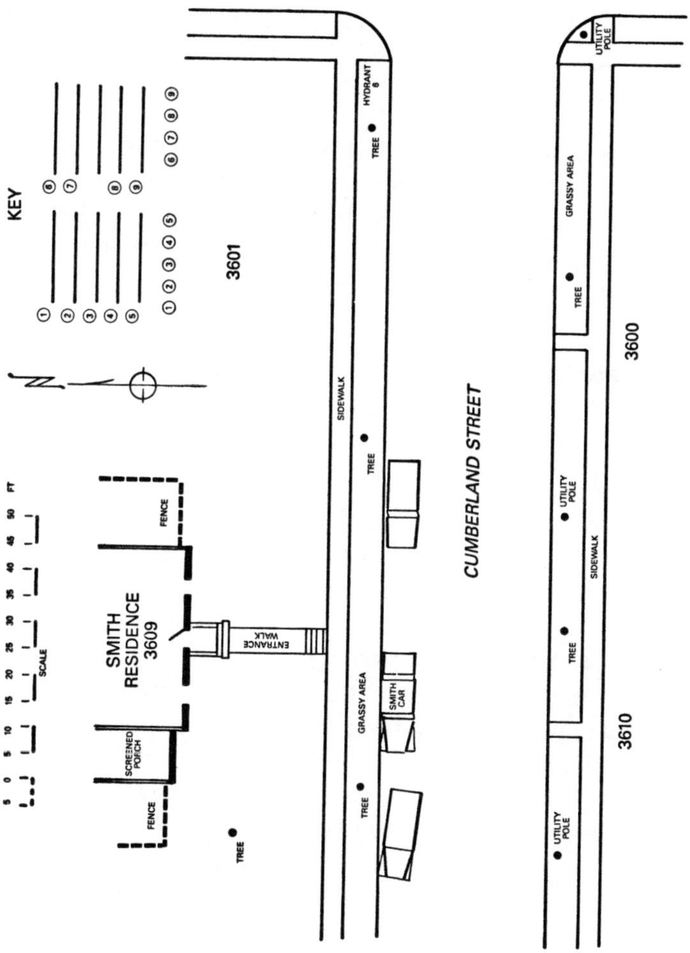

KEY
SCALE
FT
SMITH RESIDENCE 3609
SCREENED PORCH
FENCE
FENCE
ENTRANCE WALK
TREE
3601
SIDEWALK
GRASSY AREA
TREE
TREE
TREE
HYDRANT
SMITH CAR
CUMBERLAND STREET
3600
3610
UTILITY POLE
UTILITY POLE
UTILITY POLE
TREE
TREE
GRASSY AREA
SIDEWALK

Figure 4-1

evade taxes on the money. This type of case is difficult for the prosecuting attorney to explain to the jury. To assist in this task a five-foot chart showing a cycle of the money flow and the role the defendant played in this scheme was prepared. The chart was further enhanced by the introduction of color (shaded areas) to help explain the transactions. See Figure 4-2.

The presentation of this case was further simplified by the introduction of exhibits showing a very legible tax analysis sheet for each of the preceding three years. In addition to the five-foot chart, each juror was given a small copy for his or her personal reference during the trial.

Illustrate the Nature of Damages: Medical and anatomical charts are useful for all types of personal injury and wrongful death litigation to illustrate the nature of damages. See Figure 4-3.

USING MODELS TO PROVE YOUR CASE

A model can be one of the most effective pieces of demonstrative evidence in your trial arsenal when properly utilized. However, since a model in particular, and demonstrative evidence in general, is usually not direct or primary evidence in your case, but rather explanatory, illustrative or demonstrative, it is doubtful that a judge's discretion in refusing to admit it will be disturbed on appeal. This fact requires you to prepare courtroom models with the most air-tight foundation that can be constructed.

Foundation Considerations

First and foremost among the considerations that you must keep in mind is the fact that a proper foundation must be laid for the use of a model. There are several criteria that, if you adhere to them, should

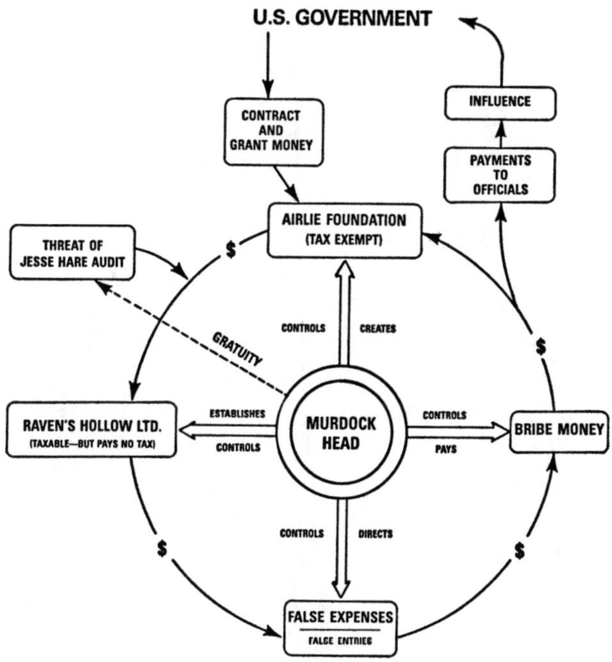
U.S. GOVERNMENT
CONTRACT AND GRANT MONEY
INFLUENCE
PAYMENTS TO OFFICIALS
THREAT OF JESSE HARE AUDIT
AIRLIE FOUNDATION (TAX EXEMPT)
$
CONTROLS
CREATES
GRATUITY
$
RAVEN'S HOLLOW LTD. (TAXABLE—BUT PAYS NO TAX)
ESTABLISHES
CONTROLS
MURDOCK HEAD
CONTROLS
PAYS
BRIBE MONEY
CONTROLS
DIRECTS
$
$
FALSE EXPENSES
FALSE ENTRIES

Figure 4-2

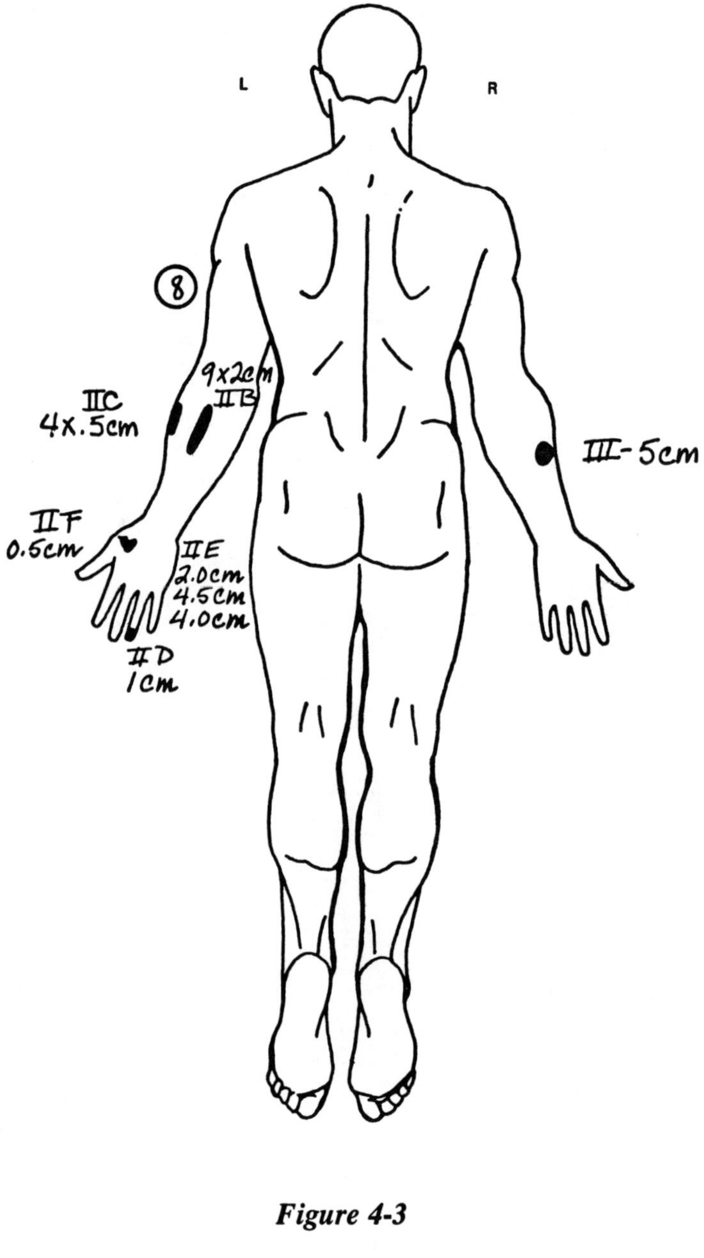
L
R
8
9x2cm
IIB
IIC
4x.5cm
III-5cm
IIF
0.5cm
IIE
2.0cm
4.5cm
4.0cm
IID
1cm

Figure 4-3

effectively meet most foundation objections, regardless of the purpose for which you are using the model. They are:

- Model prepared according to scale;
- Model verified by witnesses as reliable and correct representation of areas, object or item in issue;
- Model of such a nature so as to explain verbal testimony;
- Model of such a nature so as not to mislead the jury or cause confusion or undue influence;
- Model prepared identical with original except as to size;
- Witness qualified to testify regarding accuracy of model;
- Nature of testimony such that reference to prepared model is necessary to the jury's clear understanding of the testimony.

Assuming that the model is relevant and material to litigation and is prepared according to the foregoing formula, it should be admissible. Because of the wide discretion allowed judges concerning admissibility, you must prepare your model following the tightest possible evidentiary standards. Unless the model that you are proposing to use is required to be built to scale, models of geography, vehicle paths, buildings and machinery should, if practicable, be built and presented to the court for illustrative purposes.

Laying the foundation for admissibility should begin early in your case when the physical evidence is still in existence or before there are physical changes to geography or structures that are integral to the model. Obviously, changes or destructions could preclude construction of a model.

Should You Use a Model?

The preparation of a model is essentially a cost/benefit proposition. Before embarking on the potentially costly process of constructing a model, you should consider whether or not your case would benefit from its use. Assuming that the use of a model will necessitate its construction, as opposed to a model already being in existence, you should try to determine whether or not a model will aid the jury in understanding the case.

Implicit in this decision is the question of whether a model will be of more aid to your opponent than to you. For example, defendants may be more likely than plaintiffs to use models, because the cost is usually beyond the resources of the plaintiff. If the plaintiff has a technically complex theory and you are representing the defendant, your model may prove to be the best way for the plaintiff to prove your client's liability.

If you determine that the risks are outweighed by the benefits, you must next determine the purpose of the model. This is all-important because the purpose for which you are going to use the model determines its construction. If you are going to attempt to re-create an event you might require an in-scale model, while if you are simply going to use a model as an illustrative aid you might not need such a tight scale. This decision depends in large part upon the facts of your individual case.

If possible, however, you should opt for the use of a model as an illustrative aid because there can be difficulties in both building scale models, as well as introducing such models into evidence.

Trial Considerations in Using Models

Aside from the actual construction of a model, you should take into account several practical matters when considering the use of a model:

- ☐ If the model is to be used for scale purposes, a metal tape measure, yardstick or ruler should be modified by being re-painted and scaled so that measurements can be taken directly from the model without the necessity of translating inches to feet. This technique is especially useful if the model is one covering a large geographic area or a large physical structure (e.g., highways, bridges, industrial machinery).

- ☐ If the model covers a large geographic area and uses miniatures of vehicles that are rendered practically invisible due to the scale, larger and more visible miniatures should be prepared and used in connection with the actual miniatures. All such miniatures, whether in or out of scale, should be made out of fluorescent orange plastic to assure maximum visibility.
- ☐ You should consider using photographs of the model—either in addition to the model itself or, after the model is admitted, in lieu of the model. Effective photographic use of models and miniatures is demonstrated by the movie industry (e.g., "Star Wars").
- ☐ A pointer should be available in order to maximize line-of-sight access to the model.
- ☐ Steps should be taken to ensure that the logistics of the courthouse and courtroom permit use of the type of model contemplated. Included within these considerations are the size of the courtroom, size of the courtroom doors, size and location of the elevators, etc. Assuming a model is otherwise admissible, it is embarrassing, if nothing else, to find that it won't fit into the courtroom because you didn't measure the doors before the model was constructed.
- ☐ A "foundation package" should be assembled that includes either stipulated or certified copies of all charts, diagrams, maps, documents, and the like that were used in connection with construction. If appropriate, photographs should be taken during the construction process in order to document how construction took place.
- ☐ In connection with ensuring that the trial record is complete and in order to ensure a complete appellate record, an 8½″ x 11″ photograph of the model should be offered into evidence. Obviously, this will permit easier reference to the model in briefs.

The use of photographs for this purpose is independent of any other photographs used at trial along with the model.

When Do You Use a Model During Trial?

The question of when a model is most effectively used during a trial depends upon several factors including:

1. The complexity of the case;
2. If representing a defendant, whether opening statement has been reserved; and
3. Whether there has been a stipulation regarding the admissibility of the model.

As a practical matter, any hearing and determination relative to the admissibility of a model will be outside the presence of the jury. Such hearings will usually occur before trial.

Assuming a model is either stipulated to be admissible or ruled to be admissible, and unless its relevancy is limited to a narrow portion of the case, you can very effectively use a model during opening statement. This is especially true in tort cases which may involve eyewitnesses or questions in which physical locations are important. For example, in an automobile product liability case involving a gas tank explosion, models of the accident site as well as the auto and gas tank might be used.

Whether you are plaintiff or defense counsel, you can probably make effective use of such models during the opening statement when telling the jury about the various witnesses and what they will be testifying about. When that individual witness later testifies, his use of the model provides a continuity with both your statement to the jury as well as the testimony of other witnesses.

Obviously, the question of whether or not you use a model

during opening statement or, in fact, whether or not you use a model at all, is not a question to which there can be a single answer. It is dependent upon the facts of your case and the manner in which you intend to present those facts.

Examples of Effective Models

The descriptions of the models which follow are from actual tort cases. I hope they will serve to spark your imagination.

Example #1: An unusual number of deaths due to unexpected breathing failures were being reported at the Veteran's Administration Hospital at Ann Arbor, Michigan. There were over fifty of these incidents during a period of several months, while this type of death was found to occur about once per year in other hospitals surveyed. It was also noted that most had occurred in the Intensive Care Unit during the 4 P.M. to midnight shift.

Two nurses were charged with injecting six of these patients with a powerful muscle relaxant drug, known as Pavilon, resulting in their deaths. A scale model was prepared of the areas of the VA Hospital involved.

The model was constructed to a scale of three-quarters inch to the foot which showed interior rooms with furniture included. Each piece of furniture was attached magnetically to permit tilting the model for members of the court to view. It was used to clarify locations of patients and medical personnel and to demonstrate the line of sight to emergency light signals.

Example #2: While docked at the Brooklyn Army Terminal, the USNS James E. Robinson was the scene of an accident. The longshoreman involved suffered injuries when he was crushed between a steel pontoon and a winch. He later claimed certain winches, booms and equipment on the ship were unseaworthy and sought damages of $750,000.

A scale model was constructed which included a portion of the ship where the accident occurred. The deck and riggings were made operable to demonstrate the action that took place around the scene of the injury. The model was built to a scale of one-half inch equals one foot, and included an adjacent dock to indicate the relative elevation of the dock to the ship's deck as the tide changed.

Example #3: A scaled model of an airport including surrounding terrain was constructed for use in an aviation aircrash trial. Travel to the site was impractical so a topographic map was used as the background for constructing the model.

The airport model was built to show relative locations of airport runways and buildings. It was constructed on a scale of one inch to one hundred feet.

Example #4: While conducting a surveillance at the scene of a gangland funeral in New York City, a Special Agent of the FBI was jumped by five hoodlums and assaulted. Following the arrest a scale model was constructed showing the churchyard where the assault occurred and the streets bordering this property. The model was intended to depict how each subject participating in the attack moved around the area on that day and at what point each bit of action occurred.

The model was built one-quarter inch to the foot.

EXPERIMENTS AND COURTROOM DEMONSTRATIONS

You should constantly be on the lookout for ways to more effectively and dramatically present facts in an understandable and persuasive fashion. In certain cases, the use of an in-court experiment or demonstration can admirably fulfill this purpose. Medical malpractice cases, slip and fall cases, product liability cases, admiralty cases and the whole panorama of factual situations which give rise to tort litigation typically have some aspect to them which lend themselves to a demonstration or experiment in the courtroom.

At least once during your career as a trial lawyer, you are going to be tempted to conduct a demonstration or experiment which will either dramatically prove a point or result in discrediting a witness. As you see this technique utilized on television, it may involve a scientific experiment, a demonstration of the witness' estimate of time or distance, an experiment focusing on the witness' powers of observation or, perhaps, the reenactment of an event directed at proving the improbability of the witness' version of the event.

Foundation Considerations

There are several basic tests which you meet in order to lay the proper foundation for a demonstration to be admissible:

- The experiment or demonstration which you intend to do must be calculated to aid the jury in understanding, simplifying or clarifying evidence or issues. Thus, you must show that such evidence is supplemental to and not cumulative of the testimony of other witnesses or of other evidence.
- The proposed experiment or demonstration must meet the basic evidentiary tests of relevancy and materiality.
- You must show that the person conducting the experiment or demonstration is qualified to do so and that any equipment or apparatus involved in the experiment or demonstration is of the proper type and in working order.
- Most importantly, you must establish the conditions under which the experiment or demonstration is made. A showing of "substantial similarity" to the conditions and facts existing in the case is the general requirement.

While experiments and demonstrations can be highly effective techniques for dramatically presenting evidence in a courtroom, a substantial risk exists when you do not adequately take into account the use to which opposing counsel may be able to put your demonstration on cross-examination.

Example of a Damaging Experiment: Consider the case of an electrical engineer who built an elaborate device to conduct an in-court experiment during the rebuttal phase of evidence aimed at showing the jury that an electric motor failed to operate at 1,800 revolutions per minute (rpm).

On direct examination, the witness demonstrated that the motor operated at less than 1,800 rpm. To illustrate that fact, he utilized a pulley and purple-colored fan blades attached to the motor to induce a drag. If allowed to go unchallenged, this position was directly contrary to unequivocal testimony presented by the other side as part of its case, namely, that the motor would not operate at less than 1,800 rpm in normal operation.

After eliciting admissions that no pulleys or fan blades were associated with the motor in actual operation, they were removed and the experiment repeated using a Strobotac to measure the rpm. The results clearly proved that the motor operated at 1,800 rpm until it went off completely at low voltages. The questioning proceeded as follows:

Question: Now, would you turn the power setting on your voltmeter down to 90 volts?

(Brief pause)

Question: Do you have that?

Answer: Yes.

Question: Now, this is the [normal] operating voltage of this motor, 90 volts?

Answer: Yes.

Question: Is the yellow tape motionless?

Note: The yellow tape was a reference point on the motor shaft. So long as it remained motionless with the strobotac operating, the motor was operating at 1,800 rpm.

Answer: Yes.

Question: And is the Strobotac set at the 1,800 point?

Answer: Yes.

Question: Would you turn your voltage meter down to 70 volts?

(Brief pause)

Answer: All right, it is at 70.

Question: Is the yellow tape motionless?

Answer: Yes, it is motionless.

Question: Is the Strobotac at 1,800 rpm?

Answer: Yes.

Question: Would you turn your voltmeter down to 60 volts.

(Brief pause)

Answer: All right. It is at 60.

* * * *

Question: What is the Strobotac set at?

Answer: 1,800.

Question: So even at 42 volts the motor is still running at approximately 1,800 rpm, is that right?

Answer: Yes.

Question: You can turn this off.

Judge: Drop it to 40 and see what happens.
Note: By now the judge is curious.

Question: Okay.

Answer: All right. It is at 45.

Question: Is the tape still motionless?

Answer: Yes, it is still motionless.

Question: Is the Strobotac reading 1,800 rpm?

Answer: Yes.

Question: Drop it to 40, sir.
(Brief pause)

Answer: All right, it is at 40 volts.

Question: Do you see the tape there?

Answer: No, but the fact that I can't see it means that it is not rotating.

Question: What does it read?

Answer: 1,800.

Question: So even at 40 volts the motor is still operating at 1,800 rpm, is that right?

Answer: That is right.

* * * *

Note: The witness was now asked to go back to 100 volts and reduce the voltage again. The purpose of this was to emphasize to the jury what they had seen.

Question: Again, you are starting at 100 and dropping it down through the various voltages by manipulating the voltmeter dial?

Answer: Yes.

Counsel: I might observe for the record, your Honor, that the tape is motionless.

Question: You are now down to approximately 50, sir?

Answer: 52.

Question: Okay.

Answer: 50, 45, 40, 35, 31, 30.

Question: Okay. Would you leave it at 30? What is happening to the tape, sir?

Answer: The tape is remaining stationary.

Question: What is the setting on the Strobotac?

Answer: No. The tape is moving very slowly.

Question: What does that indicate?

Answer: It means that it is moving slightly off synchronous speed.

Question: And the synchronous speed is designed to operate at 1,800 rpm?

Answer: Right.

Question: Can we find out, by manipulating the Strobotac, what it is operating at?

Answer: I think it is moving so slowly that—As a matter of fact, it is remaining stationary now.

Question: So it is still at approximately 1,800 rpm?

Answer: Yes.

Question: Would you take your voltmeter down to 25 volts?

Answer: (Indicating.) 28, 27, 26, 25.

Question: What is the tape doing now, sir?

Answer: The tape is remaining stationary.

Question: What is the setting on the Strobotac indicating?

Answer: 1,800 rpm.

Question: Will you take it down to 20 volts?

Answer: (Indicating.) 22, 21, 20.

Question: What is the tape doing now, sir?

Answer: The tape is remaining stationary.

Question: Is the motor still running at 1,800 rpm, according to the Strobotac?

Answer: Yes.

Question: Take it down to 15 volts, please.

Answer: (Indicating.) 17½, 15 — And you had better not operate it —

Question: What happened sir? The motor stopped, didn't it?

Answer: Yes. The motor has stopped. May I turn it off?

Question: Yes. Sir, doesn't that indicate that this synchronous motor operates at 1,800 rpm, as it is designed to operate, or it doesn't operate at all?

Answer: No. You see, we applied no drag whatsoever to the motor.

Question: Well, sir, the motor, as it exists in [actual operation] has no fan blades such as you put on top and no wooden pulleys, does it?

Answer: That is correct.

Question: And the only thing that the motor operates is the 150 hertz side and the 90 hertz side blades; is that correct?

Answer: That is correct.

Question: And those are the two sets of blades that your motor was operating at a consistent rpm of 1,800 until it stopped; isn't that correct?

Answer: Yes.

Counsel: I have nothing further.

Judge: All right. Thank you.

The lesson to be learned from this type of trial occurrence is the inherent risk you run that an experiment or demonstration may backfire and prove to be the undoing of the case it was meant to prove.

Trial Considerations in Conducting Experiments and Demonstrations

In addition to the foundational requirements that are essential to the successful use of experiments and demonstrations, you should be aware of the number of other practical and logistical considerations.

- An experiment or demonstration may be more effective if it is performed outside the courtroom with video tapes, motion pictures or photographs of the experiment or demonstration utilized in court. Obviously, certain types of demonstrations or experiments are, as a practical matter, not susceptible to being conducted in court (i.e., vehicle accidents).

Even with respect to those that can be conducted in the courtroom, you should give consideration as to whether or not a video tape, motion picture or photographs would be a more effective means of presenting the experiment or demonstration to the jury. For example, video tape allows the experiment to be replayed or, through the use of freeze frame capabilities, to be frozen at a particular point as you or the witness describes what is occurring.

Video tape, motion pictures and photographs can also be effectively used by you to focus the jury's attention on desired elements of the presentation and avoid unnecessary lulls in the trial while equipment is set up or reset or problems are corrected. Even if performed in court, you should have video tapes, motion pictures or photographs of experiments or demonstrations available for marking into evidence to accompany verbal descriptions.

- Depending upon the nature of the experiment or demonstration, you may need an expert to actually conduct it in the courtroom. In this regard, you should give careful consideration to whether or not either you or an opposing witness, as part of cross-examination, should conduct the experiment or demonstration.
- As basic as it may seem, make sure that the conditions being assumed for the demonstration or experiment are consistent with the facts (e.g., pulleys, belts, and "purple fan blades").
- Rehearse the experiment or demonstration out of court a sufficient number of times to allow your attention to be devoted to the presentation.
- Moot court the experiment or demonstration prior to using it in court.
- As with the use of models, the layout of the courtroom and the lines of sight should be taken into consideration to assure visual accessibility to the experiment or demonstration by the judge and jury.

Given the right case and the right set of circumstances, the advantages of an effectively prepared and presented experiment or demonstration can be compelling. Equally compelling can be the damage done on cross-examination when an ill-prepared or ill-thought out experiment or demonstration is turned around and utilized as a weapon against the theory it was supposed to support.

"Black Boxes" in Court

Frequently during litigation there is a question regarding the operation of some mechanical device. For example, in an automobile case the operation of the speedometer might be an issue; all types of mechanical or electronic devices may be at issue in products liability cases; in aviation tort cases the operation of aircraft instruments may be at issue. It is not at all uncommon in such circumstances to bring the device in question into the courtroom so that the jury may actually see the device and relate the testimony to what is alleged to have occurred.

Any time that you are dealing with the operation of such mechanical or electronic devices, it can be difficult to verbalize how those devices operate within the context of the facts of the case. For example, in aviation tort cases, it may be extremely difficult to verbalize how aircraft instruments perform and behave in flight. This is compounded by the fact that the typical jury would not have any aviation experience. This same sort of situation is repeated in medical malpractice cases where juries may not have any familiarity with medical devices or electronic instruments; products liability cases where there is a possibility that the jury has had no exposure to the products in question, and other types of cases which involve a product, device or instrument that the average person is not typically exposed to on a regular basis.

The use of in-court experiments and demonstrations is an effective way to remedy this problem and effectively present your case. First and foremost you must recognize that the jury probably knows little or nothing about the area of litigation in which you are dealing. Such an assumption, although not always true, is the safest possible premise upon which to proceed. Highly simplified verbal explanations, photographs, and motion pictures or video tapes can be helpful. For depicting the movement, behavior or operation of instruments or mechanical devices, motion pictures or video tapes are preferable. However, even those have the disadvantage of being somewhat remote to the jury. "Black box" demonstrations can best educate the jury if it is possible to bring the device into the courtroom.

MOTION PICTURES AND VIDEOTAPE AS DEMONSTRATIVE EVIDENCE

Motion Pictures versus Videotape

The use of video medium in the legal environment most often takes place during the deposition process. Because one of the essential elements of live testimony in the courtroom—the ability to make character judgments—is preserved through the use of motion pictures and videotape, this medium provides a natural blending of legal procedure and electronic technology. However, videotape can serve a much broader purpose in the area of demonstrative evidence.

Trial lawyers have been utilizing motion picture film as a trial aid for a long time. In many ways, videotape is nothing more than an extension of motion picture film. However, there are several benefits of using videotape over motion picture film.

- Videotape can be "edited" in the courtroom without the cutting and splicing that accompanies motion picture film. This can be accomplished through the use of a digital counter-unit on the videotape playback equipment.
- You do not have to turn off any courtroom lights in order to playback videotapes.

- Videotape may be frozen at any frame of particular interest, re-wound with minimum difficulty and played fast forward in a search mode.
- Videotape requires a minimum of worry about physical logistics because playback monitors can be strategically located around the courtroom.

A Major Advantage of Videotape: In many ways, overshadowing all the practical and logistical advantages which you can derive from videotape is the very fact of television itself and, for better or worse, the inherent trust that seems to be associated with the message it delivers to people. People in general are comfortable with television and are accustomed to receiving, in most instances, reliable information from it. Accordingly, a major factor which you can take advantage of in using videotape resides in the psychological effect of the medium itself.

A Technical Overview of Motion Picture Film and Videotape

The 16mm motion picture is the industrial standard—it can be photographed and projected normally, or in cinemascope, or blown up to 35mm for projection. It has the advantage of a standard projector that is universal worldwide.

Videotape production in another story and can be as involved as film production. Don't be deluded into the notion that because you can use a 35mm camera, a super 8mm movie camera or a home video camera that you can easily operate your own video set up.

When using color, which is preferable, video color cameras must be set up with three color guns, black and white levels, front and back porches for the video signal and other parameters—and should be done with an oscilloscope. Black and white cameras are easier, but still must be set up. Whichever you use a technician is handy to have around.

Depositions are far better recorded on tape while most "show and tell" type presentations are better assembled with 16mm film and transferred to tape. Videotape can be edited, but it requires much more equipment than film editing, so initial preparation and editing on 16mm film and transfer to videotape is the way to go. Final editing of trial objections can be accomplished in the courtroom by using the digital counter on the video playback unit.

Effective Trial Uses of Motion Pictures and Videotape

Reconstructions: In any type of tort litigation involving dynamic occurrences, such as motor vehicle, train, plane, machinery or product accidents, a central aspect of the trial is frequently an attempt to reconstruct what occurred in the seconds or minutes preceding the injury.

Given the types of evidence that you may have available—eyewitness testimony, measurements, charts, survivors—the result is oftentimes less than optimal. The quality of the data available and the means of synthesizing this evidence through charts, diagrams, and models is lacking in one crucial respect. This evidence is static, while the event causing the injury is almost always dynamic.

To help fill this void, one effective use of motion picture and videotape is through animated reconstructions.

In most cases, many pieces of evidence are offered that demonstrate to varying degrees the dynamic events that caused the accident. If sufficiently reliable, and assuming proper foundation, you should have little trouble having them received into evidence. Such evidence may include charts, maps, witness statements or observations, reconstructions of occurrences based on computer data or witness observations, voice recordings, pictures and the like.

While all of these items describe the same occurrence, each does it from a different perspective. The animation/reconstruction process combines all of these elements into a single graphic depiction of the relevant moments preceding the accident.

> ***An Example of Videotape Reconstruction:*** This technique was successfully applied to aviation tort litigation by showing the jury a videotape that lasted approximately three minutes. Depicted on the top third of the television screen was an animated overhead view of the aircraft flight path as it moved. The next third of the television screen was a matching animated side view synchronized in movement to the overhead view. The final third of the television screen was a printed transcript of the synchronized sound track of the communication among the airplane's crew and between the airplane and the ground.
>
> The use of this exhibit assimilated the various aspects of the airplane flight which had, prior to that time, been shown by a number of separate exhibits. Thus, the jury was permitted to compare the various elements of the flight as they occurred simultaneously.

The problems which you encounter in using such reconstructions should theoretically be no greater than those encountered in introducing any of the individual components into evidence. Of course, you might expect claims of prejudice or cumulativeness. The unique nature of such exhibits should outweigh these objections so long as the individual aspects of the presentation are properly prepared and utilized, since the animation/reconstruction presents nothing more than a cohesive means of displaying the various aspects of a single occurrence.

Occurrences That Can Be Reconstructed: The use of videotape animation/reconstruction can be used in other types of litigation to varying extents depending upon the source data available. For example, in ship collision cases there is usually a wide range of data available regarding vessel movement and sea and weather conditions from which a reconstruction could be prepared. The same is true in railroad accidents and, to a lesser extent, in motor vehicle accidents. Similarly, a reconstruction can also be prepared in many product liability cases.

While the details of each presentation may differ based upon the foundation information available, the general format that you follow in synthesizing different aspects of the same occurrence into a reconstruction remains essentially the same.

The unique advantage obtained through such a reconstruction using videotape is the ability to freeze frames. Witnesses may comment on what is being seen in any given frame. This ability, together with the fact that the reconstruction does not depend upon the minds of the jurors to bring together all of the individual factors which gave rise to the accident, makes this technique a very powerful tool of persuasion.

Travelogues: A second use to which videotape/motion pictures may be put is the "view" or "travelogue." The ability to view evidence is frequently limited by the fact that the evidence is not easily transportable to the courtroom. This includes physical scenes, geography, vehicles, certain products, etc. While a "view" is possible, the risk inherent in a "view" lies in allowing the jury to see too much. For instance, in allowing the view of an automobile, an accident scene, or a piece of machinery where the issues revolve around one particular aspect or component, there exists a real danger of the jury being either confused or having their attention diverted to the wrong aspect of the item under consideration.

By combining the medium of motion pictures/videotape with a view, you are able to take advantage of the strong aspects of each technique. For example, assume an accident occurred at a location inconvenient to the courtroom. In this circumstance, the "travelogue" type of videotape/motion picture view can be of substantial value. This technique takes the jury to the place of occurrence without the necessity of an actual visit. It is useful when an actual visit is impractical due to time, scheduling or logistical problems.

You must pay as much attention to the quality of the motion picture/videotape evidence as to its content. After preparing a videotape "view" or "travelogue," a scene-by-scene written description or log should be prepared for reference and narrative purposes.

The written description serves a dual function. In the trial, if keyed to the videotape unit's numerical counter, it permits easy reference to any given scene. In connection with an appellate record, the log allows the court to refer to a videotape scene without actually viewing the videotape.

"Day in the Life" Presentations: This technique is used in personal injury litigation to demonstrate what a plaintiff's typical day is like following an accident or injury.

Assume you are representing someone who has suffered a personal injury which affects his ability to function on a day-to-day basis. Having certain daily activities to which jurors can relate (i.e., eating, dressing, reading, etc.), recorded on motion picture/videotape and then carefully played back to the jury so they can see the actual effect of the injury upon the quality of your client's life, is extremely effective.

In preparing "day in the life" motion picture/videotapes, you should consider several things.

- The advantage of using videotape is the ability to freeze frames. Thus, you or a witness, preferably the treating physician, can explain in detail what the jury is seeing.
- You should not prepare a "day in the life" exhibit by staging "events." While it is difficult for anybody to behave in a normal and typical fashion with a film or videotape camera following him around, you should instruct your client that he should carry on in as normal a fashion as possible. If your exhibit appears to be staged, you run a substantial risk that it will be considered too prejudicial to be admitted into evidence.
- You should carefully edit the "day in the life" exhibit to ensure that it is cohesive and does not contain either prejudicial or

extraneous material. However, all scenes not used should be available in the courtroom for your opponent.

- The type of injury which your client has should be compatible with the preparation of a "day in the life" exhibit. Obviously, injuries such as paraplegia or loss of limbs, are readily compatible with such exhibits. However, injuries which do not have outwardly physical manifestations such as back injuries or soft tissue neck injuries, are not suitable for "day in the life" portrayals, even if you *expect* your client's injury to get worse.

COMPUTER-GENERATED DEMONSTRATIVE EVIDENCE—THE NEWEST TECHNOLOGY

The current use of computers in litigation is most widespread in connection with the organization of files and depositions, maintenance of accounting records or, in the trial setting, with the use of computer printouts in lieu of ledger books and accounting records. In tort litigation which frequently involves dynamic occurrences or human perception, the computer has unique capabilities in the areas of computer-generated reconstructions, three-dimensional visualizations, and to a lesser extent, photographic enhancement and corrections. A brief overview of these computer-assisted techniques will be helpful when considering the various alternatives available during preparation and presentation of your case.

Computer-Generated Reconstructions

One area in which the computer is particularly well-suited is the generation of demonstrative evidence that attempts to analyze the movement of many objects in a three-dimensional world. For example, in aviation tort litigation it is not unusual to be faced with the task of reconstructing an accident by using a combination of voice tapes, maps, eyewitness testimony, radar data and, on occasion, flight path data. A computer expert takes these various inputs and, depending upon their accuracy and reliability, is able to formulate an accident reconstruction, the results of which are then presented to the court with the aid of maps, charts, diagrams, motion pictures, models and, on occasion, videotape. The use of a computer-generated reconstruction adds another dimension to your demonstrative evidence.

Figure 4-4 is the end product of a computer reconstruction of a hypothetical mid-air collision. It was generated using a microcomputer plotter. The background map was made using the graphics tablet of the microcomputer. The graphics tablet is a board upon which a photograph, a drawing, or, in this case, a map can be placed. A pen is used to trace any points or outlines of interest. The location of each point touched by the pen is read into the computer.

In this instance, the location was also sent to the plotter. The plotter is a flat bed over which rides a pen that is directly controlled by the computer. The computer controls whether the pen only moves or whether it writes while it moves.

The flight paths of two aircraft are shown superimposed on the map by means of two different symbols with labels on each to indicate the time at which the aircraft occupied that position.

This same information could be displayed in quite another way. A color monitor could be hooked to the computer to display the map and symbol for each aircraft. Such a moving display might give a greater insight into the circumstances leading up to the accident.

Since the microcomputer is small and portable, it is possible to bring it into the courtroom and reconstruct the accident for the jury. An alternative is to use the computer to generate a movie or videotape of the dynamic output.

Computer-generated reconstructions can be utilized in connection with witness testimony as well as closing arguments. For example, Figure 4-4 is particularly suitable for explaining the time and distance factors that related to the occurrence of the collision. It can also be used as a reference aid during eye witness and expert testimony and to explain relative geographic positions.

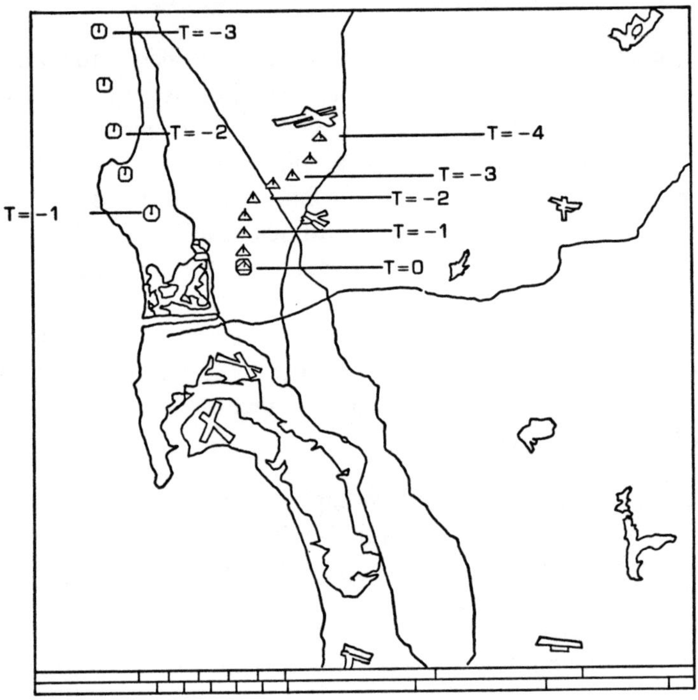

Figure 4-4

Computer-Generated Graphic Visualizations

The creation of computer-generated graphic visualizations is a technique that is particularly useful when questions of three-dimensional perspective are involved. Figures 4-5 and 4-6 illustrate the concepts involved.

Figure 4-5 illustrates a highway with two cars and a road sign. By making simple three-dimensional representations of objects of interest, the computer can be asked to present a picture of the way that the scene would appear from any particular point of view (for example, from the eyes of an observer in car #2). The question in the case (e.g., rear end collision) might be whether the road sign would have been visible to the occupant of car #2. The question is answered by the plotter output shown in Figure 4-6.

Once the computer program is written, the distances between car #1 and the sign (labeled D-1) and the distance between car #2 and the sign (labeled D-2) can be changed. If starting positions are assumed and velocities ascribed to each car, then a time sequence of pictures can be generated.

Once again, this animation can be viewed on a computer monitor, used to generate a videotape, or drawn on the plotter for the purpose of generating a movie animation. Although the objects themselves may be simplified in appearance, the perspective views will have engineering accuracy.

Computer Enhancement and Correction

There are two other computer-assisted techniques that deserve mention. They are the processing of photographs for the purposes of image enhancement or image correction.

Computer image enhancement is a process that improves the

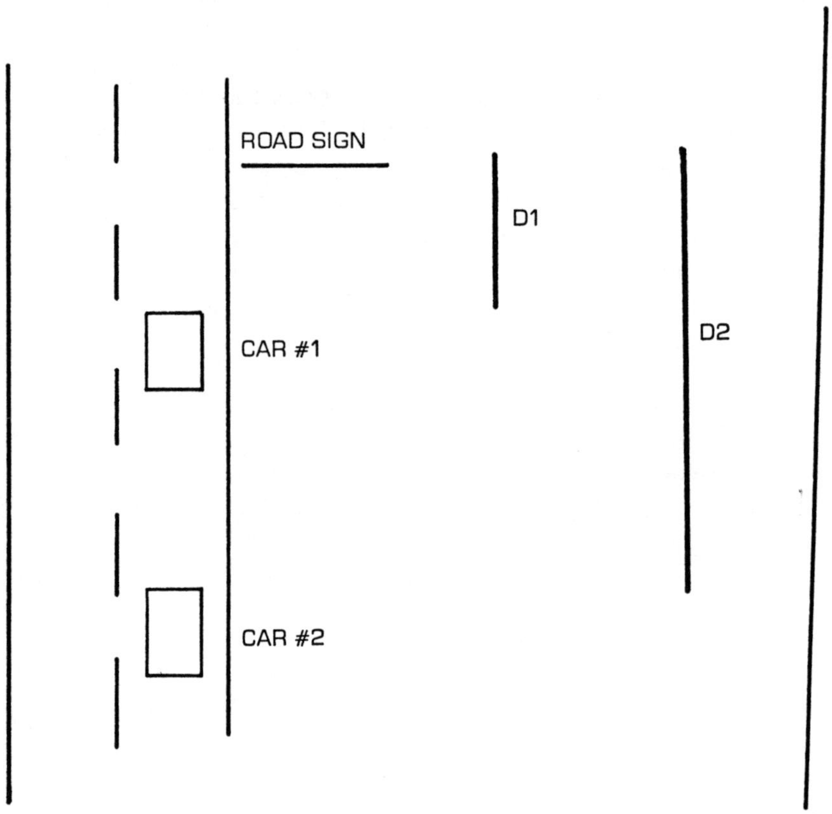

Figure 4-5

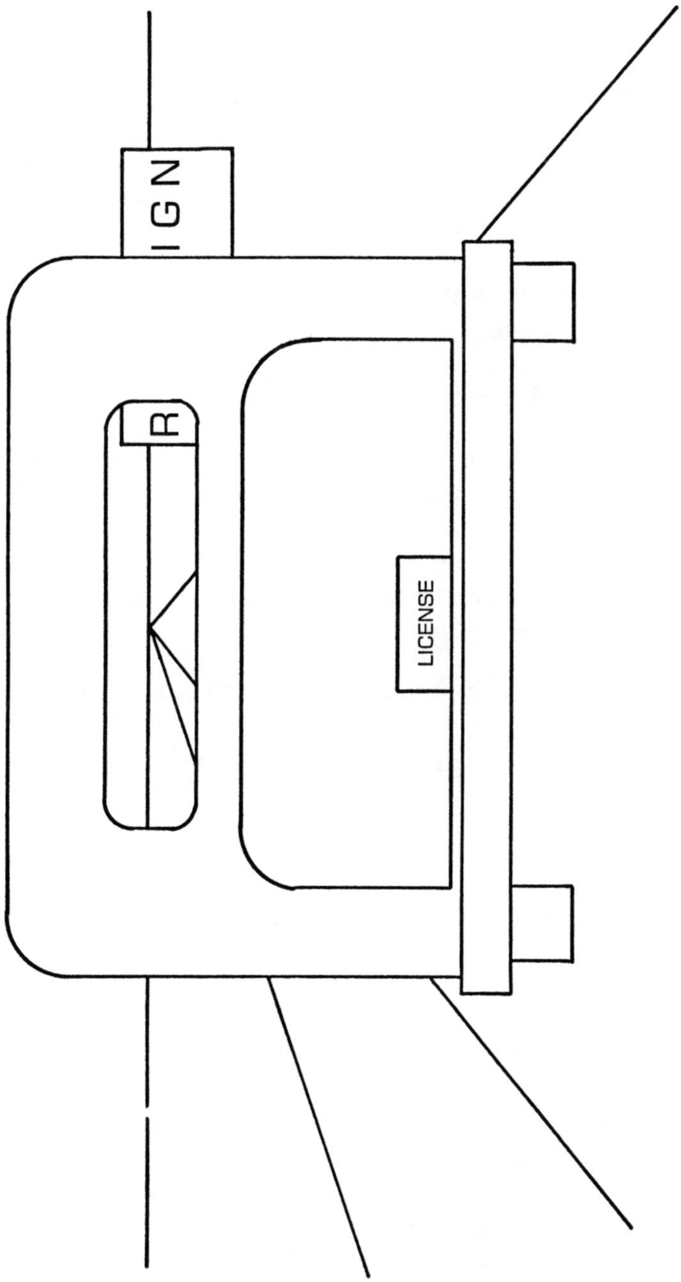

Figure 4-6

contrast of a picture. Sometimes a picture may contain information which is of such low contrast relative to other parts of the picture that it cannot be perceived by the human eye. In such a case, computer enhancement can increase the contrast so that it becomes perceptible in the computer-generated picture.

The computer can also correct defects in an image, such as those caused by misfocusing the camera or moving the camera at the instant the picture is shot. Once again, computer processing can create a photograph which corrects these images.

Like other computer-generated evidence techniques, these photographic processes are costly. Accordingly, the cost/benefit analysis becomes a significant consideration. Of equally significant concern is the fact that any utilization of the computer for generating demonstrative evidence involves the use of techniques that must, quite evidently, rely upon experts.

The knowledge that these techniques are available is something that you should bring to your evaluation of the evidence and the manner in which you can best present it to prove your case.

Trial Considerations for Using Computer-Generated Demonstrative Evidence

A number of factors must be taken into consideration in order to create computer-generated exhibits which have the maximum opportunity of being received into evidence.

- The validity of computer evidence is only as valid as the input information. If you have objective types of input information available like times, distances, locations and angles, it is probable that you will be able to meet the evidentiary standards required of demonstrative evidence of this type. If, however, you are reduced to using subjective input that is dependent solely upon witness observations and estimates, the output of such a computer-generated reconstruction will be of dubious value.

- A cost/benefit analysis must be made in order to determine whether the cost associated with such a computer process is justified by the amount at risk. This cost/benefit analysis, not unlike that made with other types of demonstrative evidence, must be made in recognition of the fact that computer-generated reconstructions have not been dealt with by the court to any great degree. Thus, unlike models, whose use is fairly well established in the court system, you are confronted with making a cost/benefit analysis without the benefit of any substantial body of judicial precedent.
- You should recognize that the creation of computer-generated reconstructions is a task that must be accomplished by experts and that those experts must be available to testify at trial.
- In using any computer-related demonstrative evidence, all foundation materials that went into creating the final evidentiary product should be available for introduction into evidence.
- A viewing should be considered during which the judge or the jury can actually see how the evidence is created. Such a procedure might be considered at a hearing on admissibility. Assuming that the judge rules such evidence is admissible, photographs of the computer should probably be shown to the jury to lend greater credibility to the evidence.

  Given the plotting and graphics capabilities of today's microcomputers, it is not unlikely that the computer-generated evidence can be created in court where various parameters can be changed to be consistent with various assumptions. This would prove to be an especially effective technique for removing some of the mystique from the computer. However, remember it also provides an opportunity for your opponent to utilize the technique to his own advantage by asking that assumptions adverse to your case be utilized.
- You should have sufficient copies of any computer-generated evidence for convenient use in the courtroom (e.g., for jurors,

judge, clerks, reporter, witnesses, counsel, etc.). There should also be at least one large blowup of the computer-generated evidence for central reference during testimony and argument.

- You should file a legal brief prior to any hearing on the evidence and its admissibility that details the applicable law, the techniques followed and the factual information relied upon for foundation purposes.

5

How To Use Expert Witnesses and Consultants for Maximum Impact

Table of Contents

5

How To Use Expert Witnesses and Consultants for Maximum Impact

WHAT CAN AN EXPERT DO FOR YOU?

It is often said, somewhat jokingly, that an expert is someone who starts out his career knowing a little about a lot of things. At some point in mid-career he knows a lot about a few things and, finally, upon attaining the status of an expert, he knows everything about nothing.

More accurately, an expert is a person who possesses scientific, technical or other specialized information who is qualified, by virtue of his or her knowledge, skill, experience, training or education to convey that information. In some cases, an expert witness may also be involved with your client, as in the case of a treating physician.

---

*The author acknowledges the contribution of Neil R. Peterson, Esq., to this chapter. Mr. Peterson, a former Department of Justice Lawyer, is a trial practitioner with a tactical and strategic sense that is second to none.

The most important element that an expert brings to his testimony is the ability to express opinions. While experts are typically thought of as being the only ones in a trial who are able to express opinions, lay witnesses may also express opinions. However, the limitation with lay witnesses expressing opinions is that, first, the testimony must be based upon the rational perception of the lay witness and, second, the opinion must be helpful to a clear understanding of their testimony or to the determination of a fact in issue.

For example, a lay witness may express an opinion about whether or not another patron in a bar, in which he was present, was drunk based upon his observation of that individual, the manner in which that individual spoke, etc. But when confronted with the results of a blood alcohol test, that same lay witness would probably not be permitted to express an opinion as to whether or not there was intoxication.

In this latter instance, the expert, by virtue of possessing scientific, technical or other specialized knowledge, can express an opinion.

What Functions Does an Expert Serve?

Basically, experts serve five possible functions in litigation.

1. On occasion, an expert may testify as a fact witness. This is most typical in personal injury tort litigation where the expert is a treating physician.
2. An expert may also testify and establish facts or data in specialized areas of knowledge. For example, an expert may testify as to the results of tests which he or she performed or observed.
3. An expert is permitted to testify as to what inference should or should not be drawn from the facts of the case. For example, what a certain blood-alcohol level means in terms of human

reaction time. In this regard, an expert may also comment upon whether your opponent's expert witness has relied upon data generally recognized by members of his profession in drawing opinions or inferences.

4. Your expert may testify as to the standards in a given area (e.g., medical standards of the community).
5. Your expert may testify about a standard of care that is either existing in your case or proposed in your case and whether or not that standard of care has been met in the facts then under consideration.

DO YOU NEED AN EXPERT?

One of the very first questions that you should ask in connection with preparing a tort case is whether or not you need an expert. To assist in making this decision, you should formulate a case plan and outline it in writing, making the appropriate changes as the case develops.

In formulating a case plan, the need or lack of need for an expert will present itself in various forms. In this regard, the following points should be considered:

- ☐ Would an expert be able to present helpful and persuasive material to the jury?
- ☐ Do you require an explanation of the general factual or technical principles in a given area that would be better handled by an expert?
- ☐ Are you going to require an experiment, courtroom demonstration or testing that cannot be done by a layperson?
- ☐ Is there an area of factual testimony (i.e., engineering data, medical testimony, etc.) that will require an expert's knowledge?
- ☐ Is there an area of testimony or factual dispute that has cause and effect implications? For example, assume you are handling an

automobile case in which your client was struck in the rear by another automobile. A question that has arisen is whether or not that sort of accident could cause certain structural damage to your client's automobile. Such an area may cause you to consider the use of an expert.

- ☐ Are the services of an expert required for what is essentially negative testimony in order to establish that a layperson is unable to testify or determine certain facts or inferences in a given matter?

  For example, assume that your opponent intends to have an eyewitness testify regarding the speed of an automobile which that witness observed while he himself was in a moving automobile going the opposite direction. In this case it may be helpful to have an expert testify that while lay testimony may be generally accurate about speeds, in these circumstances (i.e., a moving vehicle going in the opposite direction) lay testimony would not be accurate or reliable.
- ☐ One of the most basic uses of an expert, and one that mandates early consultation, is whether or not you can effectively utilize an expert to help you determine what the issues are in your case.

WHAT TYPES OF PERSONS SHOULD YOU USE AS YOUR EXPERTS, AND WHERE DO YOU FIND THEM?

In general, experts should be qualified by virtue of their knowledge, skill, experience, training or education. You should always obtain the best available expert in the particular subject matter under consideration. This may require that you retain the services of more than one expert in various highly technical cases that involve several areas of expertise. Medical malpractice cases frequently require the retention of specialists in sub-areas of surgery, orthopedics, etc. Engineering-related cases also present similar considerations.

Of equal importance is the fact that your expert should be as independent as possible. If you are representing an insurance company, it is a good idea not to utilize an employee of the insured as an expert. Clearly, such a bias or prejudice, to the extent it exists by virtue of the employment relationship, is a fertile area for questioning by your opponent on voir dire.

It goes without saying that an expert should be articulate enough to be able to handle himself effectively in the courtroom.

There are a number of sources you should consider in locating experts. Included among them are:

- Your client.
- Your client's competition.
- Government agencies (federal, state, local).
- Law firm expert files.
- University departments specializing in the area of expertise related to your case.
- Bar association files and publications.
- Retired employees of your client or client's competitors.
- Professional organizations involved in the area of expertise related to your case.

QUALIFYING THE EXPERT

Prior to an expert being able to testify in a substantive fashion, you will be required to conduct a voir dire in order to demonstrate the expert's qualifications. Following your presentation and questioning, your opponent will have an opportunity to inquire into your expert's qualifications. Assuming that your opponent has no objection to the qualifications of the expert, the witness may proceed to testify substantively.

As a general rule, the following matters should be brought out by you on voir dire:

- ☐ *All education* beginning with pertinent secondary school, college and advanced training. You should make special note of any relevant education or post-graduate type education that is especially significant to the expert's ability to testify in the area that is under consideration.
- ☐ *Formal training* by the expert including, for example, medical internships, medical residencies, grants, fellowships, etc., pointing out those which are relevant to the issues involved in the litigation.
- ☐ *On-the-job training* which is of special significance to the litigation.
- ☐ *Continuing education* such as that associated with professional seminars or conferences, papers, speeches, etc., with special emphasis on those which are relevant to the litigation.
- ☐ *Employment,* beginning with his first position and ending with the most current. You should bring out the significant duties of each job and concentrate on those where the duties are of high relevance to the subject matter of the litigation. Additionally, depending upon who your opponent's experts are, you should also, if appropriate, bring out those areas of employment that bear upon or are related to those of your opponent's expert.
- ☐ *Experience* of your expert should be demonstrated by showing not only the breadth of the expert's experience, but also the extent of your expert's involvement in special problems at issue in the litigation.
- ☐ *All professional certifications, distinctions and awards* achieved by your expert, highlighting the degree of accomplishment necessary to achieve them.
- ☐ *Professional memberships,* emphasizing those where your expert holds an elected office and those which involve selection by peer groups. This will indicate the deference and respect paid your expert by others in the field.
- ☐ *All articles, books, speeches, treatises,* etc., written and/or published by your expert making specific reference to those dealing with subjects that are of particular significance in the litigation.

In general your witness should be prepared to detail his qualifications in a narrative fashion with only one or two prompting preliminary questions by you. You should not go through a question and answer exercise because this is the area of questioning that your witness probably knows the best.

As a general rule, leading questions are permitted on preliminary matters. In the event your expert forgets something or starts to wander, you may use the leading question device in order to return him to the proper area of inquiry. In particular, you should utilize the leading question device in order to point out a specific area of your expert's qualifications that is of particular relevancy and materiality to some aspect of the case.

Assume your expert is involved in reconstruction of a rear end collision case and has done testing for the government on such collisions. After your witness testifies that he has done such testing, a good question might be "and is that testing the type involved in the accident which is the subject matter of this litigation?" Because it deals with preliminaries, this question would be proper even though it is leading.

In addition to using questions for the purpose of qualifying your expert, you should also seek to have a copy of your expert's curriculum vitae introduced into the record. Similarly, if your expert is especially well qualified you should never, if you can avoid it, stipulate to his qualifications, because the ability to testify about qualifications is important to lending credibility to your witness' testimony.

On the other hand, you should always seek to stipulate to the qualifications of your opponent's expert (assuming he is qualified). Qualification is an area which the expert should know exceedingly well, and the more you can eliminate from the presentation of your opponent's expert, the better off you will be vis-a-vis the expert's credibility.

There are a few additional matters that you should be aware of in connection with the qualification of experts:

- Some judges and juries are impressed when experts have qualifications that deal with international involvement. You should be alert to this and, if you have an expert who has had some international involvement through professional or academic groups you should be sure to point these out.
- You should always point out the number of times your expert has testified as an expert in the area in which he is now appearing. The corollary of this proposition is that if your opponent's expert has testified a number of times, you should seek to characterize him or her as a "professional expert."

  The type of approach effectively taken in this area is illustrated by the following example.

Question: Dr. Schwartz, what is ECON?

Answer: It is a consulting company, the principals of which are my brother and myself. We are both economists, and we do consulting work in that general field.

Question: Who do you consult for?

Answer: Basically, whoever retains us, where we have the expertise, the competence, and the time to do the work for them.

I work primarily in conjunction with legal actions.

Question: You basically appear in court and testify for lawyers?

Answer: We do valuation work, but it is connected with lawsuits. The actual number of times that we testify relative to the volume of work we do is quite small. I would say about 25 percent.

Question: Does the other 75 percent have to do with doing valuations for lawyers?

Answer: Yes, of that part of our work. We also do consulting work in other areas.

We have been retained over the years by a number of large and medium-sized corporations to appraise their insurance programs, their employee benefit programs, and the like.

We are involved in valuation of corporations periodically for mergers, acquisitions, dissolutions, and so forth.

Question: Where is your brother today?

Answer: He is in court.

Question: Down the hall testifying for the plaintiff in Judge Lee's case?

Answer: No, he is about 20 feet behind you.

Question: Is he present in court in the courthouse today working for a plaintiff before Judge Lee, if you know?

Answer: To my knowledge, he will be testifying on such a case in Judge Lee's court.

Question: Would I be fair in saying that your firm—that the substantial majority of the work that ECON does is to prepare valuations for plaintiffs' attorneys and appear as expert witnesses?

Answer: I would say the majority of our income comes from the legal profession. The bulk of the fees would be for valuation work rather than testimony.

Question: How much are you being paid for your work in this case?

Answer: I am being paid on an hourly basis, $50 an hour for valuation work and conference time, $75 an hour for testimony.

I don't know what the total bill will be because I don't know when I will be finished.

Question: What is the bill so far?

Answer: I don't know. There has been a partial billing only on it.

Question: What was that?

Answer: My recollection was that that was $950.

Question: At $50 an hour?

Answer: Yes.

- Frequently, and surprisingly, you will often run into attorneys who have not advised their own experts that they can be cross-examined on their qualifications. This is not unlike the trick question that, unfortunately, seems to still work today of "Have you talked to your attorney?"

  You should make your expert aware that just because you and he believe him to be an expert, accompanied with the fact that he is indeed an expert, is not sufficient for the purposes of the court or your opponent. You should be sure to advise your expert that he is quite likely to be cross-examined on the area of qualifications.

If your opponent does no voir dire of your expert you have one of two courses of action open to you. You may tender the witness as an expert and seek an immediate ruling from the court on the witness' expertise or proceed with your direct examination. If your opponent starts to examine your expert about qualifications on cross-examination, you can then object on the grounds that your opponent had ample opportunity to voir dire on qualifications and has thereby waived any right to challenge qualifications.

As a practical matter, when you have tendered a witness on voir dire, you should do one of two things: immediately voir dire and either concede the witness' expertise or challenge the witness *or* expressly reserve voir dire to be conducted during your cross-examination. The failure to reserve your voir dire may be argued to be a stipulation as to the expertise of the witness, later preventing you from challenging the qualification of the witness to testify in certain areas.

HOW TO EFFECTIVELY CHALLENGE THE QUALIFICATIONS OF YOUR OPPONENT'S EXPERT

As with any decision involving cross-examination, you should determine exactly what you intend to accomplish prior to deciding whether or not to voir dire your opponent's expert. In making this decision, you must have certain information available to you in order to be able to assess whether or not your voir dire will have the result of adding weight to the expert's credibility or, alternatively, result in undermining either the testimony to be presented or the qualifications of the witness to testify.

In assessing whether or not to conduct a voir dire of your opponent's expert, the information that you should have available includes:

- ☐ Copies of any transcripts which reflect your own previous experience with that particular expert witness.
- ☐ Any information, including transcripts, which you are able to gather from colleagues who have dealt with the expert.
- ☐ Any information available from your own experts regarding your opponent's expert.
- ☐ Copies of any learned treatises or technical publications in the area of your opponent's expertise.
- ☐ Copies of any works authored by the expert witness.
- ☐ Transcripts of prior testimony, depositions or statements by the expert in your litigation.
- ☐ Copies of school literature such as catalogues and course offerings if the opponent's qualification is in the education field.
- ☐ Copies of any professional literature or information regarding corporations, consulting organizations, etc. if the expert is engaged in that line of endeavor.
- ☐ A copy of the curriculum vitae of the expert.

Having this information available in an organized fashion, you are now able to make inquiry into the appropriate areas of the expert's background. In particular, you should keep in mind and probe in the following areas.

- ☐ Any deficiencies in the expert's education or training, as well as deficiencies in the specific area of expertise needed for testimony in the case.
- ☐ With respect to anything authored by the expert, determine whether or not he was the primary author, sole author, secondary author or merely the editor. Remember, a great many articles and publications are either "ghosted" or prepared by students or associates working under the author's direction.
- ☐ Is the witness currently practicing in the area of expertise that is in question, and is he aware of current developments in that area?
- ☐ Has the expert ever practiced in the area of expertise required for the litigation?
- ☐ What were the reasons that the expert left his various positions of employment or professional organizations?
- ☐ Has the expert stated his credentials in a misleading fashion (e.g., professor v. associate professor)?
- ☐ Has the expert ever been qualified to testify as an expert in the same area in other cases? If not, in what other areas has he testified as an expert and in what areas has he not been permitted to testify as an expert?
- ☐ Is the expert's certification (e.g., professional license) time limited and, if so, is it current?
- ☐ Is the expert a member of organizations in which election is an honor by virtue of being selected by his peers or is membership a function of merely paying dues?

You will frequently be confronted with a value judgment regarding whether or not to reserve your voir dire until the commencement of your examination of the opponent's expert. Remember, if you have a substantial amount of information to cross-examine your opponent's expert with, and believe that you have a reasonable chance of preventing him from testifying at all in a substantive fashion, you should consider not reserving your voir dire. By permitting the expert to substantially testify notwithstanding the fact that you may reserve your voir dire and cross-examine him on his qualifications, you are still permitting him to testify regarding the merits of the case. Consequently, you will be in a position of merely arguing against the weight of his testimony and not the admissibility of that testimony.

THE EXPERT AS A CONSULTANT

In addition to any trial assistance that an expert can give you in connection with proving your case in the courtroom, an expert can play a valuable role prior to trial, both as a consultant in the broad sense, and in connection with discovery.

An Expert Can Aid Issue Recognition

An expert can assist you in recognizing issues in the case and whether or not there should be any significance attached to them. Additionally, the expert can assist you in determining whether or not additional experts might be needed.

An Expert Can Be Invaluable During the Discovery Process

Interrogatories and Requests for Production: An expert can serve an invaluable consulting role by helping you formulate interrogatories to propound to the other side and in developing requests for admissions. An expert can and should review all records and documents produced by and for you. In connection with documents produced by your opponents, your expert should review those documents and determine what additional documents should be requested.

The Deposition of Your Expert: In connection with depositions, the role of an expert is extremely significant. As a general rule, unless you agree with your opponent to trade expert depositions, a court order must be entered in order to take an expert's deposition. With respect to the deposition of your expert, a number of guidelines should be observed:

- The expert should be prepared and, obviously, as substantively knowledgeable as possible. This includes his reviewing all discovery taken in the case that might conceivably be pertinent to his area of testimony, as well as any materials outside the record.
- A mock cross-examination of the expert should be undertaken that is as realistic as possible in order to prepare the expert for the deposition. Consideration should be given to videotaping the mock examination so both you and the expert can study it.
- The expert should be briefed in the same manner as any other witness regarding his manner, bearing and conduct during the deposition.
- Whenever he is faced with technical material or literature, the expert should be instructed to request an opportunity to examine it in detail before answering questions about it.
- Instruct your expert not to bring any documents or notes with him to the deposition.
- With respect to hypothetical questions, your expert should be instructed that he should not answer them unless he is satisfied that the hypothetical contains all of the facts, circumstances and conditions necessary for a complete answer.
- When your expert is being deposed, the deposition should, preferably, take place in your office. A deposition should not take place at the expert's office because there is too much ready accessibility to additional documentation. The corollary to this proposition is that you should always seek to depose your

opponent's expert at his place of business in order to have ready accessibility to documents.

Deposing Your Opponent's Expert: Just as there are guidelines to be followed when your expert is being deposed, there are also guidelines to be followed in taking the deposition of your opponent's expert. Before you begin, know why you are taking the deposition. For example, if you are simply taking it for discovery purposes, you can take a much broader approach to determine all of the information and opinions possessed by the expert. On the other hand, if you are taking the deposition for trial purposes, you want to be sure that it is in proper form and elicited in a fashion that is most favorable to your client.

- You should thoroughly explore the credentials of the expert, as well as all of the material reviewed by the expert.
- You should request that all of the material reviewed by the expert be produced at the deposition and that it be marked as exhibits.
- You should utilize the interrogatory answers provided by your opponents that required expert input or bear upon the expert's testimony as a means of cross-examining the expert and/or an outline for the cross-examination.
- When you are dealing in a case that has multiple experts, you should determine that all experts agree with one another. In this regard, you should determine whether or not the experts have conferred in order to reconcile any differences in their opinions.
- You should seek to qualify your own expert through your opponent's expert. For example, if you are utilizing an expert who is highly qualified and recognized as an expert, you may ask your opponent's expert, "Isn't it true that Dr. Smith is recognized as an expert in the field of internal medicine?"
- Wherever you can obtain agreement from your opponent's expert with facts, positions, contentions, etc., seek to do so. Frequently, you can utilize your opponent's expert to significant

advantage in your case by indicating the extent of agreement that that expert has with your position.

- Seek to determine whether the expert intends to testify at trial.
- Determine who your opponent's expert considers as authoritative in the field with respect to individuals, as well as publications. You can then determine whether or not those publications provide a basis for later impeachment of your opponent's expert at trial. You can also determine whether or not you might want to obtain one of the individuals your opponent's expert indicates is an authority as a witness for your case.
- A corollary of the previous guideline is to determine who your opponent's expert disagrees with in his field of expertise and then go out and seek to determine whether or not that individual might be a potentially valuable expert for your case.
- Determine each and every occasion upon which your opponent's expert has testified in prior cases. In this regard, you should especially probe him or her regarding areas of testimony that are similar to the one then in question. If possible, you should seek to get copies of all such trial transcripts, depositions, etc., and use them at trial.

THE EXPERT AT TRIAL

An expert witness can mean the difference between winning or losing at trial. The manner in which he presents himself, the clarity with which his testimony is presented, the demeanor with which he testifies, the use of demonstrative aids, and the overall tenor of authority which he brings to the testimony are all key elements.

Order of Questioning

Before questioning, you should cover the qualifications of your expert and establish his expertise in the field of testimony then under consideration. Following the proffer of the witness as an expert, you should elicit exactly what foundation information was reviewed by the expert prior to formulating his opinions.

Once you have accomplished these preliminaries, you are in a position to ask the expert, first, what his opinions are and, second, to explain those opinions. At this point you must determine your style of questioning.

Style of Questioning

To make the most of your expert, you must make a judgment as to the best manner for presenting your expert. In this regard you should determine if it is best to utilize a question and answer or a narrative technique of examination.

The advantage of the question and answer technique is that you have a significantly greater amount of control over the parameters of the testimony and can ensure that all the proper information is included in the witness' answers. The advantage of the narrative testimony technique is that it seems more spontaneous and allows the witness to present more of himself to the jury. The narrative style can be extremely valuable where the witness' personality is appealing. When presenting an expert witness through the narrative testimony technique, a large chart, diagram, or other piece of demonstrative evidence can serve as an outline to remind the expert of areas that should be covered.

Narrative expert testimony is especially useful with medical experts as the following example indicates.

Question: Would you tell us about your follow-up treatment of Mr. Green and his progress?

Answer: I have seen Mr. Green periodically since his injury in 1969. Over this period of time, the left arm with the fractures and the plates and the screws healed with some residual loss of motion in the wrist, with some scar and with some residual loss of motion in the forearm.

During the period of the initial six months after the injury, Mr. Green had some intermittent alteration in the feeling, and the easiest way to test that is with a safety pin, one side of which is sharp, the other side of which is dull. And if you can distinguish between the two, this is a very good method of determining the general status of the nerves in the extremity.

He had intermittent loss of sensation in the left lower extremity and intermittent loss of sensation in the left upper extremity. He also complained of considerable dizziness; and by "dizziness" I mean that when he would arise from a sitting position or bend the head forward and then stand, there was a tendency for the room to feel as if it were spinning. He also complained of pain in the cervical spine.

During the course of the treatment, we've had each of these evaluated. Doctor Houghton will speak on the dizziness problem.

When Should the Expert Testify?

When the expert testifies is as important as how he testifies. It is usually preferable to have the expert testify as the last witness in your case. This is true because the expert can be used to sum up the testimony and present opinions that are helpful to your case at a time when it is less likely that the jury will forget his opinions.

Apart from any other reason, there is a very practical reason for having your expert testify at the conclusion of your case. As a practical matter, the expert should have the benefit of relying upon *all* of the prior testimony in order to have his opinions well-founded.

The risk you run in having your expert testify at an early point in your case is that (1) he may be contradicted by later testimony from your own witnesses, and (2) the factual predicates upon which your expert testifies may not be sustained thereby taking a chance that your expert's opinions may be stricken from the record.

Dealing With Your Opponent's Expert

Should You Cross-Examine? The single most important question that you must answer is whether or not to cross-examine your opponent's expert. The risk that you always face in examining your opponent's expert is that he will have been primed to make the most important mileage on cross-examination. Indeed, this should be the very manner in which you prepare your own expert. His own testimony will be far more convincing if it is elicited by your opponent, just as your opponent's expert's testimony will be more convincing if it is elicited by you.

Techniques of Cross-Examining: In conducting an examination of your opponent's expert you should start with the voir dire. The first decision that you must make is whether to reserve the voir dire until you conduct your examination or, alternatively, conduct it prior to the direct testimony. You should then consider cross-examining the expert on the facts utilized in the assumptions. Having established the factual predicates for the expert's testimony, other than those which may have been testified to under direct examination, there are a number of types of questions that can be asked of the expert regarding substantive testimony.

Notwithstanding the approach you take, leading questions should always be used in cross-examining your opponent's expert. For example:

> **Question:** You have no idea whether Mr. Thomas had anything to do with the management of his own portfolio and if he did, how much he had to do with it, isn't that a fair statement?

Answer: That is a fair statement.

Question: Now, let's turn to the Diamond Ranch Realty. Isn't it true, sir, that your charts, as demonstrated in Exhibit 22, do not reflect in any way that Mr. Thomas owned only 80 percent of Diamond Ranch?

Answer: They do not.

Question: Is that correct, sir?

Answer: That is correct.

Question: And isn't it also true, sir, that your charts, as set forth in Exhibit 22, do not in any way show that Mr. Thomas' son devoted 30 percent or more of his own time to Diamond Ranch?

Answer: That's correct.

Question: They make no adjustment whatsoever for that, do they, sir?

Answer: They do not.

Question: And isn't it true that your Exhibit 22, those charts, make no adjustment whatever for the initial investment of $40,000 capital by Mr. Thomas, nor do they make any adjustment for the substantial amounts of further capital investments that Mr. Thomas made as testified to by his son; isn't that true?

Answer: It is true because those factors would be irrelevant in computing his earning capacity.

Question: Well, sir, wouldn't it be relevant to show what part of the retained earnings were due to his express personal services as opposed to the personal services of others or the investment of capital funds, though, would it?

Answer: Yes.

The following checklist presents some areas of inquiry that may be asked either directly or indirectly of the expert. In each case, they will either elicit favorable testimony or will lay the foundation for you to argue to the jury.

☐ *Assumptions:*

- What assumptions has the expert used?
- Are the assumptions used by the expert the proper ones?
- Is the use to which the expert put the assumptions proper?
- Would others use different assumptions?
- If so, how would the result differ?

☐ *Facts:*

- What facts were used by the expert?
- Were they the proper facts to use?
- Was the use to which they were put proper?
- What other facts should have been used by the expert, and, if they had been used, what difference would they make to the opinion?
- What changed facts should have been used by the expert, and what difference would they have made to the opinion?
- Should less facts have been used by the expert, and, if so, what difference would that have made in the opinion?

☐ *Cause and Effect:*

- Has the expert used any cause-effect relationships? If so, is the result necessary, probable, or merely possible?

☐ *Standard:*

- What standard was used by the expert? Was it a proper standard? Was its use proper?
- Are other standards available, and, if so, how would their use have affected the result?

☐ *Reasoning Process:*

- Was the reasoning process of the expert correct?

☐ *Conclusions:*

- Would other persons have reached a different conclusion on the basis of the same facts, data, and/or assumptions.

- Did the expert have enough facts, data, and proper assumptions for him to formulate an opinion?

☐ *Impeachment:*

- Check the various deposition points above and ascertain whether they are applicable in the cross-examination of the expert.
- Make sure that the expert is of the same school of thought as the person whose conduct is being called into question. This is especially important in medical malpractice cases and damage aspects of all personal injury cases.
- Is there a local standard in the jurisdiction in which the case is being tried, and, if so, does the expert know what the standard in that locality is.
- Are there any weaknesses in the testimony of the expert, especially:
  — Any writings by the expert;
  — Any speeches by the expert;
  — Any prior testimony by the expert in other cases;
  — Any indications of bias, such as always testifying on one side of an issue, for one side in litigation, or for one attorney;
  — How other courts treated the testimony of the expert. Remember, many experts who are professional witnesses have left a long track record behind them in court opinions.
- Is the testimony of the expert inconsistent with what has already occurred in your case?
  — Does it coordinate with the witness' deposition testimony?
  — Does it coordinate with the documents that have been produced in the litigation?
  — Does it coordinate with the answers to interrogatories that have been provided?
  — Does it correlate with the responses to requests for admissions that you have received?
- If the opposing expert has given an exposition of general

principles, consider asking whether he can cite any support for his exposition in the writings of others and consider asking whether other experts agree with his exposition.

Bear in mind, however, that you should have checked with your expert to ascertain that there are in fact disagreements between the opposing expert and other authorities before you ask this type of question.

- Be especially careful where the expert has given an opinion without disclosing the basis for it. Do not give the opposing expert a platform to begin his reasoning process by your cross-examination. Just bring out the defects you have noted from his deposition and leave the rest of the matter for your closing argument. Where uncertain, use leading questions to "feel out" the witness.
- Ask the opposing expert what he has reviewed prior to testifying. Demand copies of the materials he has reviewed even if he did not use them during his testimony.

☐ *Order of Examination:*

- Do not follow the opponent's order of examination in your cross-examination of his expert. To do so merely gives the expert a chance to repeat familiar territory. Mix up your questions and probe different areas in different orders to see if you can generate any uncertainty or confusion by that method.

HOW TO EFFECTIVELY USE HYPOTHETICAL QUESTIONS DURING THE DIRECT AND CROSS-EXAMINATION OF AN EXPERT

What Is the Purpose of a Hypothetical Question?

A hypothetical question asks an expert to assume certain facts and express an opinion based upon those facts. The preparation and use of hypothetical questions serves several functions, including being able to elicit favorable opinions from either your expert or your opponent's expert.

- Hypothetical question preparation requires you and your expert to agree on critical factors and issues in the case and what is needed to support related opinions.
- Hypothetical question preparation becomes an outline or a checklist for the foundation of factual elements required in order to sustain your burden of proof.
- Hypothetical question preparation serves as an outline for what additional discovery is needed by you from your opponent in order to sustain your burden of proof.
- Hypothetical question preparation requires you to determine what the appropriate legal criteria are as applicable to your case in order to formulate proper hypotheticals.

Formulating Effective Hypotheticals

A hypothetical question should be written out prior to trial in consultation with the expert. Included within it should be all relevant and meaningful facts required to properly draw the hypothetical. You need not include all the facts in the case because some are irrelevant to the opinion.

The hypothetical question will generally provide a basis for the expert to demonstrate how his opinions were formulated and how those opinions relate to the case. It will also permit the expert a basis upon which to further expound upon his opinions. For example:

Question: Assuming facts one, two, three, four and five, do you have an opinion as to X?

Answer: Yes, I do.

Question: What is that opinion?

Answer: My opinion is . . .

Question: Would you please explain that answer?

At this point the expert can go on to explain his answer in a much broader sense, relating his opinion to the specific facts of the case in detailed fashion, generally making a much more persuasive presentation. Thus, the hypothetical, if properly drawn, serves as a springboard.

All facts that you assume for the hypothetical must be proved. On occasion, certain facts can be assumed that will be later brought out in the case. However, if you do not bring those facts out in an admissible fashion, you run the risk of having your expert's opinion stricken from the record. This is one of the primary reasons for having your expert testify last at the trial. Additionally, be sure your hypotheticals are consistent with the law. Otherwise you may run into trouble.

Here is an example of what can happen if you ask a hypothetical question that isn't consistent with the law.

Question: Assume now that there is medical testimony that this same man is impaired to the extent of 50 percent of the body as a whole. Now, how would you arrive at that figure from what you had before?

Answer: Well, I would say the reasonable thing to do would be simply cut it in half.

Opposing Counsel: I'm going to object and move to strike that because the law in the Tenth Circuit specifically states that the measure of damages in this type of case is the difference between what this man will earn in the future, his earning capacity, and what he would have earned.

Judge: You are correct.

Opposing Counsel: And cutting something in half by 50 percent, in no way approaches the reality of the law in this case.

Judge: Does it?

Counsel: I don't know, Your Honor. May I approach this another way?

Judge: Yes, try again.

You should be aware that on occasion you will not be able to get an expert to testify to the full extent that you would otherwise like him to testify. In such a case, work with your expert as far as he will go and utilize your closing argument as the place to argue the inferences to be drawn from the expert's testimony. Be careful about simply telling your expert to accept something as true or he may find himself in the following situation.

Question: Let's turn to the first page of Exhibit 21, sir, which is the schedule of security transactions.

Do you know who Mr. King consulted, if anybody, relative to making any security transactions?

Answer: No.

Question: Do you know if he talked to his broker about the wiseness of buying or selling certain stocks?

Answer: No.

Question: Who was his broker, do you know?

Answer: He had several brokers.

Question: He had several brokers?

Answer: Yes, sir.

Question: And I take it you don't know whether he spoke to any, or all of them, or anybody else?

Answer: No, I wasn't in his office when he did it.

Question: Then would you explain to me, if you don't know who he consulted with respect to the management of his securities portfolio how you imputed a management fee to Mr. King personally of over $79,000?

Answer: I was requested to do so by counsel.

Question: But you have no information of your own in any of the tax returns or personal information from Mr. King that he consulted nobody at all, but he made all these decisions himself, that he never talked to his brokers; isn't that right? In other words, you were told to impute that?

Answer: That is correct.

Cross-Examining with Hypotheticals

In cross-examining your opponent's expert in the area of hypotheticals, there are certain factors that you should keep in mind.

- Hypotheticals should be objected to where they are either improper or incomplete. An objection inherently makes a hypothetical suspect.
- Ask your opponent's expert if his opinion would change if an omitted fact from the hypothetical were included. If he agrees, ask him how it would change, and, if the answer to those two questions are satisfactory, and you feel confident in your cross-examination, ask him why his opinion would change.
- If your opponent had to re-ask the hypothetical several times in order to get an answer, consider interrogating his expert as to whether or not his opinion would have changed under the different versions of the hypothetical presented to him.

Where the changes to the hypothetical were minor changes, you run the risk with this technique of appearing to quibble over words or argue with the witness. This can be an effective technique where you bring out the fact that the expert has been paid to present his opinion notwithstanding the nature of the question. Additionally, if you are able to obtain a repeated series of answers from the expert that agree with your position, there is an additional psychological benefit derived.

Here's an effective example, from the cross-examination of a medical expert:

Answer: On our last visit, there was some tenderness in the scar over the plate that was placed on the radius, which was the site of increased pain in the recent past.

Question: And you're saying that you don't know what the course of future care would be in respect to that arm, at this point?

Answer: No, sir.

Question: In other words, that's a matter of speculation at this point?

Answer: Yes, sir.

Question: Now, you've indicated that Mr. James is exercising at home under a program prescribed by yourself, sir?

Answer: Yes.

Question: Has he shown improvement since he started that exercise?

Answer: Yes, sir, he has.

Question: Has his strength continued to improve?

Answer: Yes, sir.

Question: Has his mobility or range of motion improved at all?

Answer: Yes, sir.

Question: All right, is he continuing to exercise?

Answer: Yes, sir.

Question: Is his strength continuing to improve?

Answer: Some, yes.

Question: Do you know at what point it will stop improving or is that also a matter of speculation?

Answer: That would be a matter of speculation, sir.

Ask the expert if his opinion would change if any of the facts to be shown later are not shown or are not true. For example:

Question: Doctor, assuming his motion is no longer restricted, there'd be nothing to prevent Mr. Dickens from resuming work, do you agree with that?

Answer: If it completely resolves, I would agree with that.

Question: And it's speculative as to whether it will, one way or the other?

Answer: Well, I think that we can take some reasonable certainty as to how long it takes for something to resolve, and we generally feel that if a condition continues, such as the vertigo, which is demonstrable for five years, that it's going to be permanent.

Question: Well, it has lessened, hasn't it, Doctor?

Answer: Yes, it has.

Question: So it's not demonstrable at the same level, is it?

Answer: No, it's not.

Question: So there has been a change in it, hasn't there?

Answer: Yes, there has.

Question: And the same factor which brought about that change could bring about additional changes, couldn't it?

Answer: Yes, it could.

Question: And, in fact, it could make it disappear completely, couldn't it?

Answer: Yes, that's true.

Question: Okay. When you say that, in your opinion, it was directly related to the accident, how do you know that? Were you at the hospital when Mr. Dickens was admitted in Colorado?

Answer: No, I wasn't.

Question: Were you at the hospital when Mr. Dickens was admitted to St. Francis?

Answer: No, I wasn't.

EFFECTIVE TECHNIQUES FOR STRONG PRESENTATION OF EXPERT WITNESSES

Demonstrative Evidence

There are a number of techniques that you should consider in order to dramatically heighten the presentation of testimony and evidence by your expert witnesses. The use of demonstrative evidence, such as diagrams and graphs, can be extremely helpful in explaining testimony and equally helpful in capturing and holding the jury's interest. As has been discussed in Chapter 4, on demonstrative evidence, you must have a proper foundation for the demonstrative evidence, separate and apart from any expert testimony you offer.

The extent to which the use of diagrams and charts have been accepted is illustrated by a case in which a witness in a robbery case was permitted to make a diagram on the courtroom floor of the layout of the building in which the robbery was committed. Drawings made by your experts while testifying are admissible, even if done on a blackboard which itself is not susceptible of inclusion in the record. As a matter of trial practice, however, it is better to utilize a large artist's pad in lieu of a blackboard or, if a blackboard must be used, to arrange to have photographs taken of the diagrams or other material before they are erased or replaced.

In addition to your expert witness' drawings or charts, you should also consider the use of drawings made by you while examining either your experts or your opponent's experts as graphic representations of the witness' testimony. It is this last type of graphic evidence—drawings made by you while examining an expert—that presents the most fertile area for an astute trial lawyer in the presentation of experts.

In the typical trial setting, the jury listens to the verbal testimony, reviews the evidence or demonstrative aids and retires to reach a verdict, sometimes with and sometimes without parts of the record. On occasion, the jury may be permitted to have certain portions of the testimony re-read to them. Typically, however, a jury will not be given an entire trial transcript, even assuming one is available. In any event, any material taken into the jury room rests within the sound discretion of the judge.

Considering these circumstances, the beneficial effects of preparing an expert witness' testimony in graphic form and then having it received into evidence is apparent. Not only are you then able to have a tangible record of the testimony before the jury, but you can also use it during your closing argument.

This technique has been fully described in Chapter 4 and is an especially effective manner for presenting an expert's testimony.

Use of Affidavits

A technique that can be used to minimize the effective impact of a strong adverse expert is the offering of direct testimony of that expert, including voir dire, by way of affidavit or statement, with only cross-examination being conducted live. By doing so, the strong expert who would otherwise make a substantial impact on direct examination is lessened and more tightly controlled through the use of leading questions and cross-examination.

An added benefit is that the court, assuming it adopts this procedure to expedite the trial, will oftentimes require pre-submission of direct testimony affidavits or statements by counsel, thereby allowing additional preparation time.

The offer of qualifications and direct testimony through affidavits or statements might be accomplished as follows:

Question: Doctor, I show you a document entitled Plaintiff's Exhibit No. 28 for identification. Can you identify the document?

Answer: Yes, sir. That is my resume of experience.

Plaintiff's Counsel: If there is no objection, I would like to offer this.

Defense Counsel: No objection.

Judge: It will be received.

Question: Doctor, I show you a document entitled testimony of Dr. John W. Johnson, marked Plaintiff's Exhibit 29 for identification. Can you identify that?

Answer: Yes, sir, it is my written testimony.

Plaintiff's Counsel: I will offer that as Plaintiff's Exhibit No. 29.

Defense Counsel: No objection.

Judge: It will be received as Plaintiff's Exhibit 29.

At this point, the witness is subject to cross-examination where leading questions can be utilized.

This technique can also be utilized to maximize the effectiveness of weak experts. You may often find yourself confronted with an expert who is well qualified, but will not make a good impression on direct examination, either because of his demeanor or because he is not a well-spoken individual. Just as frequently these individuals are extremely capable of defending their opinions on cross-examination. By suggesting the utilization of affidavits as a means of offering qualifications and direct testimony, you are in a position of presenting your expert in a semi-protected form.

Qualifying Your Expert Through Your Opponent's Expert

Another effective technique for both qualifying an expert and adding additional credibility to his testimony is through the opposing expert. For example, if you are able to elicit an admission from your opponent's expert that your witness is an expert or, better yet, the leading expert in a given field, the testimony of your expert becomes more credible. While such an endorsement is certainly not determinative, it is at least helpful.

Questioning might proceed along the following line:

Question: Now, sir. Do you know Dr. John W. Smith?

Answer: Yes, sir, I do.

Question: And he is the individual who has been sitting next to me at counsel table?

Answer: Yes, sir, he is.

Question: Sir, do you recognize him as an expert in the field of x-ray analysis?

Answer: Yes, sir, I do.

Question: And, sir, isn't it in fact true that he is considered to be the leading authority in this country in the area of x-ray analysis?

Answer: Yes, sir, I believe that is correct.

As with any witness, the effective presentation of expert testimony requires careful preparation and presentation. In a society where litigation is becoming increasingly complex and is dealing with a wider range of technical issues, one characteristic which separates experts from lay and percipient witnesses is that experts are, presumably, the most knowledgeable individuals in the courtroom on the subject matter in controversy. Your job is to ensure that you present their expertise in the most effective and persuasive fashion.

INDEX